MW00694882

ADVENT

FOR

EXILES

Caroline Cobb

ADVENT

FOR

EXILES

25 DEVOTIONS
to Awaken Gospel Hope
in Every Longing Heart

B&H
PUBLISHING®
BRENTWOOD, TENNESSEE

978-1-4300-9584-2

Published by B&H Publishing Group
Brentwood, Tennessee

Dewey Decimal Classification: 242.33
Subject Heading: DEVOTIONAL LITERATURE
/ CHRISTMAS / ADVENT

Cover and interior illustration by Stephen Procopio. Ribbon foil texture by Anoottotle/Shutterstcok. Author photo by Michelle Bill.

1 2 3 4 5 6 • 27 26 25 24

For Ellie, Harrison, and Libby. May you always find your home in God.

Contents

PART I
THE FIRST EXILE

PART II
IN THE DARKNESS OF EXILE, A SUNRISE

PART III
IN THE WILDERNESS OF EXILE, A SEED AND A HIGHWAY

Preface

In the fall of 2020, I released *A Seed, A Sunrise*, an album exploring the ache of Advent, the joy of Christmas, and the expectant yearning for Christ's return. Most of the songs on this project grew out of spending extended time in the book of Isaiah in 2019. Though I cannot fully explain why, the prophet's use of metaphor and imagery and his message of hope for the exiles rings all sorts of bells in my artist heart. For me, this seems especially true when I couple the poetry of Isaiah with the season of Advent.

Although I wrote and recorded the album just prior to the troubles of 2020 (I distinctly remember thinking how strange it was that people were wearing masks in the airport on my way home from recording in Nashville in February), these songs of hopeful longing took on a deeper resonance by the time of their release in October of the same year. In addition to the upheaval and isolation wrought by the COVID-19 pandemic, we were facing a divisive political landscape, a struggling economy, civil unrest, and what felt like near-constant exposure of injustice and darkness—both on the nightly news and, sadly, in the church itself. The year 2020 had shaken our idols, uprooted our comforts, confronted us with our mortality, and brought a new awareness of the brokenness around us. If Advent is a season of groaning and ache, then 2020 had felt like Advent all year. One long, painful groan.[1]

To me, *A Seed, A Sunrise* felt like the right kind of "holiday album" for 2020. As an independent artist, I held no fantastical notions of climbing the charts or dominating the radio airwaves with this album. Spoiler alert: it did not! Songs drawn from Isaiah exploring the theme of exile don't exactly scream "commercially viable" anyway. In music and now writing, commercial viability has never been the goal; I want to steward the stories of Scripture, help people rehearse the hope of the gospel even in the darkest moments, give them true words to pray and sing to God.

My hope for the album was simple: "I pray that this album will be a balm for us and a resource for the church, giving voice to both longing and hope," I wrote in an article I published just before it's release. "As this difficult year draws to a close, Advent gives us the opportunity to voice both the unwavering hope we have in Jesus and the longing cry, 'How long, O Lord?' And when that long-awaited Day of rejoicing comes, it will be all the more glorious for the ache we experience now, like the dawn after a long darkness, or a distant garden blooming in the desert."[2]

Meanwhile, I had promised patrons of *A Seed, A Sunrise* I would write a devotional book for them as a supplement to the album. In 2021, I finally got to work on this "side project." But in the writing, I discovered the album had barely scratched the surface for me. I wanted to dive deeper into the poetic imagery of Isaiah, draw more connections between our current experience and the biblical theme of exile, help readers imaginatively engage in the ache of Advent as a way of expanding their joy at Christ's coming. Over time, the supplemental "side project" became a serious, primary work, and the book you are reading now, *Advent for Exiles*, is the fruit of more than two years of writing and wrestling this deep dive into words.

This devotional is written for those who have felt—or at least feel ready to acknowledge—the long groan of exile. The veil on our aching hunger for home may have lifted in 2020, but the years following have not done much to take the edge off. We need Advent companions willing to recognize the darkness around and within. Only then will we be able to fully rejoice in the arrival of Jesus, the Light of the world. I pray *Advent for Exiles* will do just that.

Introduction

The Old Testament tells the story of two tragic exiles.

In the first chapters of Genesis, God casts Adam and Eve out of Eden and stations cherubim with flaming swords to guard the way back. Years later, Assyria and Babylon would carry God's people into captivity, far away from the Promised Land. Each of these exiles came on the heels of disbelief and sin, God's people failing in their mission to mirror and expand his glory to the world. Banished east of Eden and east of the Promised Land, they were helpless to save themselves or make a way back home to God.

But in each of these exiles, God gives a promise of hope: a bright *sunrise* chasing away the shadows of night, a *seed* sprouting green in the desolate wilderness, a *highway* leading them home, a good *king* who will shepherd his lost sheep with justice and sacrificial love, and an Edenic *city* where God will make his home with us forever. Before and beneath each exile, a God who redeems and restores is at work. And in each exile, a faithful remnant waits in hope, watching eagerly for God's promised salvation.

Advent is a season set aside for a similar waiting and watching. Even as we count down the days to Jesus's first arrival at Christmas, we also anticipate his promised second arrival, when God will bring his exiles home and the curse of sin and death will be undone at last.

Like the faithful remnant in exile, we scan the horizon looking for the sunrise to break brightly into all this darkness. We wait for the seed sprouting green out of the dirt, making all this barren wilderness into a glorious garden. We watch for King Jesus to come in glory and reign forever. During Advent, we stir up our anticipation for the arrival of Christ—both his first *and* his second. With intention, we make ready so that we might welcome the day of his coming with joy: *At last! At last!*

Advent for Exiles is designed to help you make ready. Its primary aim is to whet your appetite for the coming of Christ.

But I must be honest: this book is not a feel-good read filled with the warm fuzzies we often associate with Christmas. In these pages, you will not find "the most wonderful time of the year" but thorns, ashes, and deep gloom. You'll meet Adam and Eve homesick for Eden and the weeping exiles in Babylon hanging up their harps in the poplar trees. But as the darkness of a long night augments our longing for the sunrise,

I hope these images of exile will expand your desire for the promised Messiah and amplify your joy at his coming.

At last! At last! Our Savior! Our way home to God!

THE THREADS IN A TAPESTRY

I had been writing this Advent devotional on and off for more than a year but still had trouble with the "elevator pitch." In explaining what I was working on to friends and supporters, I kept using descriptors like "mash-up," but it never felt right. Words like this made it sound like I was throwing a bunch of random ingredients in a bowl, hoping against hope that something resembling a cake might come out of the oven in the end. I kept searching for a description that would hold two seemingly opposed facts: this devotional would be comprised of many strands but was meant to be one cohesive, interconnected piece.

That summer, I took a break from writing to hit the road for our family's annual summer vacation. The five of us were taking a self-guided tour of the Biltmore House in Asheville, North Carolina, when I finally found it—the elusive word for which I had been searching. Halfway through our tour, I noticed a large tapestry displayed on the sitting room wall, and the light bulb went off. *That's it!* I remember thinking.

The Advent devotional is like a *tapestry*. Many threads woven together. One grand, beautiful picture.

At least seven essential threads are woven into *Advent for Exiles*: the season of Advent, the metanarrative of Scripture (with a special focus on Isaiah), the theme of exile, biblical imagery and metaphor, music and lyrics, narrative storytelling, and responsive exercises. Although these seven threads are meant to be taken as one whole, perhaps it would be helpful at the outset of this book to pull out a few and describe them separately.

ADVENT

The word *Advent* is derived from the Latin word *adventus*, which means "coming." In the English dictionary, *advent* is synonymous with words like "arrival" or "appearance." The first season in the traditional church year calendar, Advent is designed to be a season of preparation and anticipation, the stoking of an ever-growing expectation for Christ's arrival—both his first and his second.

In her book *Advent*, Fleming Rutledge points out the season's unique orientation to time: "The other seasons in the church calendar follow the events in the *historical* life of Christ—his incarnation (Christmas) . . . his path to crucifixion (Lent), his passion and death (Holy Week), the resurrection

(Easter) . . . the descent of the Holy Spirit (Pentecost)."[1] But, Rutledge argues, Advent holds both the past and future; we *look back* at Jesus's first coming, even as we look *forward* to his coming again. Even more, the season helps us see the reality of the church's present: "In a very real sense, the Christian community lives in Advent all the time. . . . Advent contains within itself the crucial balance of the now and the not-yet that our faith requires. . . . In that Advent tension, the church lives its life."[2] Advent is a season set aside for looking backward and forward, but it also invites us to recognize the tension we feel in the space between.

Before you begin this devotional book, I would like to make a confession: my experience with Advent is somewhat limited. Most of my life as a Christian has been spent in "low church" spaces, and for a long time, I viewed Advent and Christmas as one long season. For this reason, I will not pretend to be an expert or even a seasoned practitioner.[3] Instead, I view myself as an artist who has seen something beautiful, good, and true in the liturgy and ethos of the Advent season. I can't help but try to paint it for you so you can experience it too.

EXILE

In 722 BC, Assyria conquered the northern kingdom of Israel. By 586 BC, Babylon's defeat of the southern kingdom of Judah was complete as well. Most of God's people were taken captive, forced to live in exile. The ones who stayed behind felt an "exile" of another sort, living amid the rubble and ruin of their former life.

But this was not the first experience of exile we see in Scripture, nor would it be the last. The exilic longing for home is a biblical theme that runs from Genesis to Revelation, from the fall of Adam and Eve (Gen. 3) to John's vision of God making his home with us forever (Rev. 21:3). As citizens of heaven, we will still experience a sense of exile until the day of Christ's return (1 Pet. 2:11). According to Hebrews 11, we are "foreigners and temporary residents on the earth," homesick for a heavenly city to come (Heb. 11:13–16). Exile is synonymous with estrangement, displacement, longing, and an apt analogy for the "already but not yet" tension of Advent. By putting ourselves in the shoes of the Old Testament exiles and by acknowledging our own sense of homesickness, we are participating in an Advent disposition and awakening our anticipation for Christ's arrival.

THE BOOK OF ISAIAH

The book of Isaiah has been called "the fifth Gospel." In it, we find the problem of sin (Isa. 1:1–31; 5:1–30), the atoning work of the Messiah (Isa. 53), and the promise of "new heavens and a new earth" (Isa. 65:17–25). Isaiah's ministry began an estimated seven hundred years before the birth of Jesus and ended about 120 years before Judah's exile. Even still, his message would be profoundly comforting and relevant for both the Old Testament exiles and followers of Jesus today.[4]

As a literary work, I believe Isaiah is best taken as a mosaic rather than a straightforward speech, logical treatise, or chronological narrative. If you are a linear thinker, you might even find Isaiah frustrating as the book swings from image to image, from oracles of judgment to proclamations of good news. But if you are willing to view the book with the eyes of an artist, I think even the most linear among us will find a deep well of beauty in its pages. In *Advent for Exiles*, I have taken a "mosaic" or an "artistic" approach to this complex Old Testament book, drawing on Isaiah's imagery as an essential organizing principle, as illustrated in the section titles.

POETIC METAPHOR AND BIBLICAL IMAGERY

Poet Emily Dickinson writes, "Tell all the truth but tell it slant. . . . The Truth must dazzle gradually/ Or every man be blind."[5] Biblical metaphors help us grasp the truth of one thing by bringing it into conversation with another, often highly visual thing. For example, the concept of sin takes on new layers of meaning when Isaiah compares it to a waterless garden, an unfaithful wife, or a filthy rag. The exile is even more devastating when it is pictured as a desolate wasteland, scorched and dry and overgrown with thorns. The people's longing for a Davidic king is more potent when mapped onto the visual of sheep, scattered and vulnerable without a good shepherd. The Bible is dripping with metaphor, imagery, and poetic language. This devotional book picks up several of those metaphors for a closer look, in order to help you grasp the truth of the gospel with both your head and your gut.

THE ARTISTIC APPROACH

C. S. Lewis famously said, "Reason is the natural organ of truth, but imagination is the organ of meaning."[6] As a storytelling artist often "in her feels" who also values rigorous Bible exegesis, I deeply resonate with Lewis's statement. Again, I believe Christians need both, often in tandem. The "threads" of this book are designed to engage "organs" of both reason and imagination. My hope is the use of biblical imagery, music and lyrics, storytelling, and physical or visual exercises might stoke the ember of your imagination into flame, even as the Bible readings and biblical principles within the reflections anchor you, giving boundaries for that fire.

Since I have already confessed to not being an expert on Advent, let me also say at the outset that, even though I have spent much time in God's Word, I am not a seminary-trained theologian or Bible scholar. At the core, I see myself as a storyteller. And God's Story is the most beautiful, most deeply true story I have ever come across.

HOW TO READ THIS DEVOTIONAL

The book itself is divided into eight sections, all of them a "thread" in their own right. As you read, you might notice a loose pattern: the first seven sections begin in the brokenness of exile but move forward day by day into the hope of Jesus our Messiah. On each day, you will find a song lyric, a Scripture reading, a reflection, and a prompt to respond—either in prayer or in some physical practice. Again, these elements are meant to engage your mind, your imagination, and—in some cases—even your physical body.

By definition, a devotional is not an academic textbook. It is an invitation to engage with God relationally, not just collect more information about him. With this in mind, I encourage you not to skip over the songs, Bible readings, or responsive exercises. You can listen along to the songs by visiting http://carolinecobb.com/adventforexiles and even take them with you as you go about your day.

As I sing often, "I'm a steward of the Story as the moon reflects the light. So if you see him and forget me, I've told this Story right."[7] And I pray it is so with this Advent devotional. May these pages help you rehearse, remember, and respond to the good news of Jesus and stir your anticipation for his glorious arrival!

A Note to Parents and Families

As a parent, I am always looking for ways to connect the content from my personal devotional time with our family's devotional practices. In fact, my desire for synergy here is so strong that in the process of writing the proposal for this book, I briefly considered writing a devotional geared toward families rather than adult readers. So, although this book is written primarily with an adult reader like you in mind, my heart is for the children in your life as well. I am praying your interaction with the stories and truths within this devotional might somehow spill over in service of your family's Advent experience.

My hope is that parents and caregivers find the imaginative elements within *Advent for Exiles* particularly helpful—that the music, biblical metaphors, and responsive exercises might spark meaningful conversations and hands-on, embodied experiences for you and the children in your life. As you consider how to integrate the content of this book with your family's time around God's Word, allow me to offer three prompts and ideas utilizing these imaginative elements:

First, over the course of the Advent season, your family could listen to each of the 16 songs in the book, taking time to discuss the lyrics and the Scripture that inspired them. As Paul reminds us in Colossians 3:16, music and singing has a way of helping God's Word "dwell richly" within us. Music can also easily be incorporated into everyday life: you might listen and discuss on the drive to school in the morning, as you make dinner in the kitchen, or as you tuck everyone into bed each night.

Second, consider guiding your family through the biblical metaphors we explore in this book: home and homesickness, hunger and feasting, light and dark, wilderness and garden, ruin and re-building, a lost sheep and a Good Shepherd. As I wrote in the introduction, I believe biblical imagery and metaphor help us grasp biblical truth in deep ways. And in my experience, children seem to be especially captivated by story and image.

Finally, I believe the responsive exercises within this devotional book contain embodied activities well-suited for children and adults alike. The exercise at the end of day 4, for example, prompts you to wake up early to wait for and savor the sunrise. Day 7 asks you to cut a branch off a living plant and watch it for several days as you consider what it means to abide in Jesus, the "Righteous Branch." And day 23 prompts you to savor a meal in light of the heavenly feast we will experience when Christ returns. Instead of doing the various responsive exercises by yourself, I encourage you to invite your entire family to participate. In fact, your experience will likely be all the richer having seen how the children in your life respond! You might also come up with your own embodied activities based on the daily Advent readings.

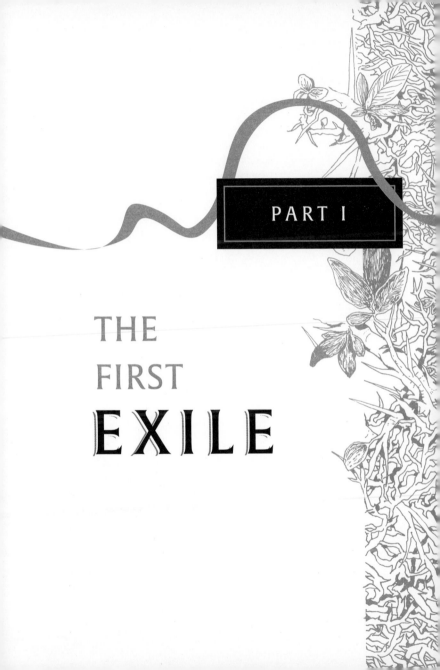

PART I

THE
FIRST
EXILE

For you I'll plant a garden
And fill it with light
Food for your mouth
And colors for your eyes

And I will breathe into the dust
The breath of life and all my love
And when you open your eyes
You will see and be satisfied
Because I will be with you

I will be with you
I . . .

from "Garden"
by Caroline Cobb

16

Imagine Eden

Read Genesis 2:5–25

Can you imagine Eden?

The garden is just *bursting* with beauty and light, the creativity and abundant goodness of God on full display. Picture creatures as wildly diverse as the platypus and porcupine, baboon and butterfly. Catch the scent of a thousand flowers springing up like miracles from the soil. Watch as the vibrant sunset paints the sky orange and pink. Can you imagine reaching up to take hold of fruit weighing heavy in the trees, taking a bite, feeling its juice dribble down your chin? Can you hear the babble and splash and roar of a great river branching into four more? And—oh the wonder of it!—God himself has made his home there, walking among the trees. Eden shimmers with his sacred presence.

And it was good.

And yet, Scripture tells us the pinnacle of God's creative work comes on the sixth day, when God makes the first human beings. Genesis 2 uses intimate language: the Creator bending low to breathe life into the dust, forming and shaping our first parents like a potter at the wheel. The Lord had declared the sun and stars good, the animals and plants good, but now he speaks an emphatic "*very good*" (Gen. 1:31)! Then, God gives Adam and Eve a special designation and mission: to bear his image as little mirrors of his glorious light, goodness, and kingly rule.

Theologian Meredith Kline notes that just as Eden was meant to be a habitation for God—a first temple—so too human beings were to be like little temples where God would dwell.[1] As *imago Dei*, Adam and Eve were commanded to "fill the earth" with more and more of God's presence, expanding the boundaries of Eden's garden temple until his goodness and glory covered the whole world like a canopy.

Paul expounds on the *imago Dei* motif in Ephesians 2 by calling us God's "workmanship" (v. 10), a word translated from the original Greek *poiēma*. Like poetry, we are meant to host and express the heart, wisdom, and nature of God, just as the masterpieces of Bach, Shakespeare, and Michelangelo speak of their makers. We are God's artwork! His song! His poem! As humans, our meaning and mission, our dignity and joy, are bound up in our Creator.

But we are not meant to image God alone. As Paul continues in Ephesians 2, he uses striking language to speak about the church, mixing agricultural and architectural metaphors. Individual *poiēma* are built together into God's house, laid like living stones upon Jesus the cornerstone. But then, God's house does something buildings usually do not do: it begins to grow. Together, the church "*grows* into a holy temple in the Lord . . . built together for God's dwelling in the Spirit" (vv. 19–22, emphasis added). Just as Adam and Eve were like little temples, God means for his people to be a garden temple, a dwelling place for his sacred presence expanding ever outward like Eden, until the whole earth is filled to bursting with his glory![2]

Put yourself in Adam and Eve's shoes for a moment. Can you imagine the unflagging joy, peace, and utter *delight* they must have felt? Gardening without thorns or weeds. Work without toil. A relationship untainted by insecurity or ego. The abundant beauty of creation unspoiled by decay or death. Here in Eden, Adam and Eve could mirror and expand God's presence as his *poiēma*, without the smear of sin or the warp of self. Here in Eden, they could dwell in the unfiltered light of God's presence, without shame casting its familiar shadow.

In Eden, Adam and Eve were totally at home with God, and God—oh the wonder of it!—had made his home with them . . . and *in* them as *imago Dei*. There was no sense of separation, no lack, no longing for something better. *At least not yet.* There is only brimming-over beauty, overwhelming goodness, and the all-satisfying presence of a loving God.

Like Adam and Eve, you too were made for this abundant life with God. As a human, you are hardwired to find your home in God and for God to make his home with and in you. As his beloved *poiēma*, you are designed for worship—a life oriented toward expressing his worth and beauty. As St. Augustine prayed, "You have made us for yourself, and our heart is restless until it finds rest in you."[3] In a sense, the "good life" we keep searching for is found back in Eden. We are made to live in the all-satisfying presence of God. Nothing else will quite do, and we know it deep in our bones.

RESPOND IN PRAYER

God, when I imagine the beauty and
goodness of Eden—your abundant love
as Father, Son, and Spirit flowing over
into everything you made—I am full of
awe and delight. And I am homesick too.
I long to be completely at home with
you, fully present, without the distortion
of sin and self. I am made for you. God,
even as I am homesick for Eden, you
have called me your *poiēma* through
Christ. Help your people bear your image
until the whole earth is filled with your
glorious presence. Amen.

A broken mirror, painted black
There is no light reflected back
Thorns grow up where there was green
All sorrow, shame and broken things

Paradise has barred its doors
It's guarded by the flaming swords
We can't go back, we can't go back

We wait, we wait for you!
Come with your light!
We wait, we wait...

---

from "We Wait for You"
by Caroline Cobb

Shame the venom running through my veins
A curse, a cancer and my death
And every child of mine
Will feel the serpent's bite
But one will crush his head
Oh come and crush his head!

---

from "Eve's Lament"
by Caroline Cobb

Imagine Exile

Read Genesis 3:1–24

It's tempting to rush through the next part of the story: Adam and Eve's terrible choice, the banishment from Eden, the long-lasting consequences. Uncomfortable with dissonance, we want to jump ahead to the resolution. But in doing so, we reduce the fall to just another plot point, a little bump in the road on the way to a happy ending.

For Adam and Eve, the fall was no mere plot point. It was a *tragedy*. A catastrophic uprooting, an unnatural wrenching, a ruin seemingly beyond repair. The Maker banishes his beloved *poiēma* from the garden and from his full presence. The entrance into Eden would be guarded by the flaming sword of the cherubim. There would be no way back.

Can you see Adam and Eve stumbling away in shame, looking back over their shoulders at those swords ablaze? Can you feel the surge of horror as they realize what they have done? The deep regret, the fear of the future? *Oh, what have we done?*

Instead of reflecting God's glory to the world, the image bearers were like broken mirrors painted black, curved in on themselves.[4] Instead of living and working alongside each other in a flourishing garden, their work and relationships would be marred by "thorns and thistles" (3:18). Instead of God's presence spreading over the face of the earth, their sin and shame would instead "be fruitful and multiply" (Gen. 1:22, 28 ESV), creeping like a shadow into every corner of creation.

In her poem "Success Is Counted Sweetest," Emily Dickinson describes how loss and deprivation sharpen our appreciation and longing. "Success is counted sweetest to those who ne'er succeed," she writes, "To comprehend a nectar requires sorest need."[5]

Somewhere east of Eden, Adam and Eve were feeling "sorest need." See them toiling and pushing, arguing and blaming, ever so homesick for the garden. They had feasted on the abundant goodness of God, and now they hungered for even just a taste of what they had before. Our first parents must have felt their need acutely, just as we know how much sweeter a nectar would taste after days and days without a meal. The reality of their exile was ever present, like the ache of an empty stomach.

And yet even as they longed for Eden, they knew returning would mean facing those fearful angels and their fiery swords of judgment. Going back meant certain death, a death their sin deserved. *We can't go back. We can't go back.* Even on their best days, this truth hung heavy over them like a funeral shroud:

We can't go back. We can't go back.

Even as we imagine Adam and Eve's exile, we must consider: *our exile from God is no less real. Our need is no less acute.* Because of our sin, we dare not approach the garden gate, those cherubim with swords on fire. Because of our sin, approaching the dwelling place of God's presence without a mediator would lead to certain death. We are incurably banished, chronically homesick. For you and me, the curse of sin is no little bump in the road. It's a *tragedy*.

We can't go back. We can't get in.

Just wait a moment here. Resist the temptation to fast-forward to the happy ending. Let yourself *feel* the homesickness, the weight of sin on your shoulders, the hunger pangs. Let yourself *see* the cherubim barring your way to God. When we allow ourselves to linger in the dissonance and ache of exile, we amplify the glory of what God has done in the advent of Jesus.

For even as exiles longing for Eden, Adam and Eve had reason to hope. God had promised *a seed*, a son of Eve that would come to crush the serpent's head and redeem all they had lost in the fall. To the snake, God declares, "I will put hostility between you and the woman, and between your seed and her seed. He will strike your head, and you will strike his heel" (Gen. 3:15 HCSB).

Do you hear the good news here? Their story is not over. Their exile would not last forever, and their tragedy would be redeemed somehow. Adam and Eve did not understand then, but we know now: Jesus is the seed of the woman, the Son born to utterly defeat the serpent, crushing its head. Jesus is the better Adam, the perfect *imago Dei* as the "radiance of God's glory" (Heb. 1:3 HCSB) and "the exact imprint of his nature" (Heb. 1:3 ESV). Jesus is God's presence coming out of Eden to find us in our exile and bring us home. Through

Jesus, God would somehow transform the fall into a feast and our banishment into a banquet.

So Adam and Eve waited. And during Advent, you and I are invited to wait—even ache—alongside them. We link arms with our first parents, homesick for God's full presence and longing for the promised seed to come again.

RESPOND IN PRACTICE

Consider fasting from a meal today or, if this is not possible, schedule a food fast sometime this week. Use the time you would usually be eating to meditate on the reality of our exile from God's presence, and respond in prayer. Let your physical hunger and deprivation pique an increased spiritual hunger for Christ's coming. Let the rumblings in your stomach whet your appetite for God. And when you break your fast, remember to savor and take it slow. Let each delicious bite remind you how sweet and satisfying the second coming of Jesus will be when he returns at last.

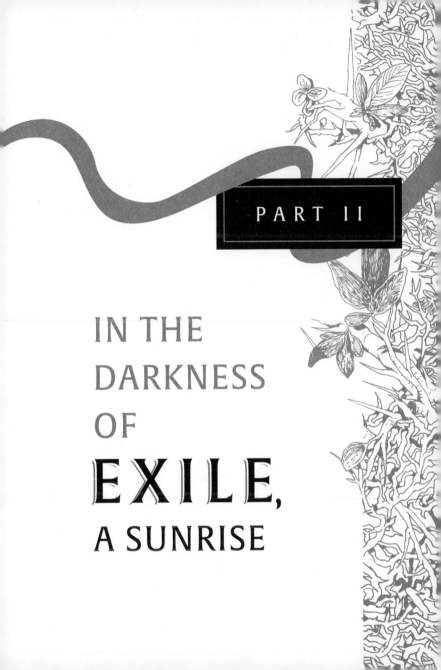

PART II

IN THE
DARKNESS
OF
EXILE,
A SUNRISE

A forest cut down by the axe
Like the end of the story
When it's all turned to ash

But up from the stump
The bud of a flower
A seed of hope in the eleventh hour

---

from "We Wait for You"
by Caroline Cobb

Exile from a Second Eden

Read Isaiah 1:1–9, 16–20

Centuries later, God's people find themselves in the Promised Land, a sort of Eden 2.0: "a good and spacious land, a land flowing with milk and honey" (Exod. 3:8).

Even Solomon's temple echoed Eden, with blossoming flowers carved into its cedar walls and pomegranates engraved on its pillars. The lampstands were likely modeled after the tree of life, and gold and onyx—found in the garden—decorated both the sanctuary and priestly garments. (Exod. 25:7, 11, 17, 31–40). Cherubim with fiery swords were carved into the wooden ark of the covenant and embroidered on the thick curtain outside the holy of holies, "guarding" these symbols of God's presence just as they guarded Eden's gates after the fall. For an ancient Jew, walking into the temple would have been a visceral experience. Bible teacher Nancy Guthrie writes, "When the Israelites walked into the temple, it took them back—back to the beauty of the house God had built so long ago, that initial outpost of heaven, the garden of Eden."[1]

And just as Adam and Eve were meant to mirror and expand God's glorious presence to the world around them, God intended the Hebrew people to do the same. Theologian Michael D. Williams notes that "God calls Israel to image God, to represent his character and rule in the world."[2] These were the people of the Red Sea split in two! The pillar of cloud and fire! Water gushing from the rock, the thunder and trumpet and smoke of Sinai, the glory shining on the face of Moses! Their ancestors saw the walls of Jericho crumble and the giant Goliath fall. They were heirs of God's covenant promises to Abraham and David, redeemed to be his "treasured possession" and a blessing to the world (Deut. 7:6 ESV; 1 Pet. 2:9; Gen. 12:2–3).

But even in Eden made over, God's people fell short. Generation after generation. Again and again.

> "Oh sinful nation, people weighed down with iniquity.... They have abandoned the LORD; they have despised the Holy One of Israel; they have turned their backs on him." (Isa. 1:4)

For God, Israel's ongoing sin felt deeply personal. Consider the highly relational metaphors the prophets chose before and during exile: God has been a generous Father; they are rebellious, faithless children (Isa. 1:2; 30:9). God has been an attentive Vinedresser; they are a vineyard yielding only bitter grapes (Isa. 5:1–4; Jer. 2:21). God has been a loving husband; they are an adulterous wife who just can't seem to stop cheating (Jer. 3:1–8; Ezek. 16; Hosea 1:2). They have continually *abandoned* his ways. *Despised* him. *Turned their backs.*

In his compassion, God has patiently sent prophet after prophet to warn and exhort his beloved people.[3] And yet his people continue to break covenant, turning to powerless idols and disobeying his commands. God is slow to anger, but he is also just.

And so, when the prophet Isaiah asks, "How long should I shout warnings to these people?" God's reply is stark:

> Until cities lie in ruins without inhabitants, houses are without people, the land is

> ruined and desolate, and the LORD drives
> the people far away, leaving great emptiness
> in the land. . . . Like the terebinth or the oak
> that leaves a stump when felled, the holy
> seed is the stump. (Isa. 6:11–13)

Like Adam and Eve, God's people would once again be sent into exile because of their unfaithfulness. The Promised Land—this Eden made over—would deteriorate into a desolate emptiness and ruin. The people would be cut down, a small remnant left like a stump—a grievous reminder of a tree that once stood strong and tall.

The desolation Isaiah describes became reality when Assyria conquered the northern kingdom of Israel around 732 BC, and Babylon did the same to Judah a few generations later (2 Kings 17:6; 25:1–21). The Eden-like temple was burned with fire, and Israel's adversaries were "like men in a thicket of trees, wielding axes, then smashing all the carvings with hatchets and picks" (Ps. 74:5–6). As a final blow, the prophet Ezekiel has a vision of God's glory-cloud departing from the temple and from the threshold of Jerusalem, a tragic symbol of God no longer dwelling among them (Ezek. 10:18–19). By 587 BC, God's temple was a heap of rubble and ash, and almost all of the Hebrew people had been carried off into foreign lands (Jer. 41:4–5).

When Jeremiah saw the destruction of Judah, he frames it in de-creation terms, a reversal of God's "let there be light" in Genesis 1:

> I looked at the earth, and it was formless and
> empty. I looked to the heavens, and their
> light was gone. (Jer. 4:23)

Oh, what a contrast! Rather than *Eden remade*, this is *Eden undone*. Exile is de-creation, a reversal of the light, beauty, and blessing we saw in day 1 and Genesis 1–2. As the screen fades to black, these are the last images we see: the stump of a great tree chopped down, a world filled with darkness and ruin.

But do not miss the promise God makes to Isaiah, even in the pronouncement of exile: "the holy seed is the stump" (6:13). Like Adam and Eve before them, God's faithful remnant would look to a promised seed: a tender shoot growing green out of the stump of a seemingly dead family tree. Despite all evidence to the contrary, their story is not over. And so, in the darkness of this exile from the second Eden, they believe God's promise, keeping their ears open and their eyes on the horizon. They are longing to hear the voice of God speaking "let there be light" once again. In Advent, we join them saying, "We wait for you! Come with your light!"

RESPOND IN PRACTICE

As an exercise, find a windowless room and turn off the lights. Sit in the darkness until you begin to feel uncomfortable, then sit a bit longer. Set a timer if you need to. In the darkness, acknowledge and confess your desperate need for the Light of the world, praying aloud, "God, in the darkness, we wait for you. Come with your light." Pray it many times, emphasizing different phrases.

But from the shadows the sun will rise
The people in darkness will see a great light
We're longing, praying for the dawn

We wait, we wait for you!
Come with your light!

from "We Wait for You,"
by Caroline Cobb

People living in the darkness!
Lift up your head and see the sun
I see a new day dawning
It brings good news for everyone.

I see the sun rising!
I see the sun rising!

from "Pave Every Road"
by Caroline Cobb

DAY 4

A Light in the Darkness

Read Isaiah 8:22–9:7

"They will look toward the earth and see
only distress, darkness, and the gloom
of affliction, and they will be driven into
thick darkness." (Isa. 8:22)

"We hope for light, but there is darkness;
for brightness, but we live in the night.
We grope along a wall like the blind; we
grope like those without eyes. . . . For our
transgressions have multiplied before you,
and our sins testify against us."
(Isa. 59:9–10, 12b)

In *The Two Towers*, the second novel in Tolkien's Lord of the Rings trilogy, Frodo and Sam find themselves driven into the thick darkness of Shelob's lair, deep in the mountains of Mordor. "They walked as it were in a black vapor wrought of veritable darkness itself that, as it was breathed, brought blindness not only to the eyes but to the mind, so that even the memory of colors and of forms and of any light faded out of thought. Night always had been, and always would be, and night was all."[4]

Perhaps God's people in exile felt like Frodo and Sam: thrust into thick darkness and "the gloom of affliction," groping blind along the cavern walls as memories of their life in the Promised Land faded into black. *We can't go back.*

The prophet Jeremiah certainly felt this way: "He has driven me away and forced me to walk in darkness instead of light. . . . He has made me dwell in darkness like those who have been dead for ages. He has walled me in so I cannot get out" (Lam. 3:2, 6–7).

Hear the prophet's gut-wrenching grief as he mourns for Jerusalem and her people:

> Joy has left our hearts; our dancing has turned to mourning. The crown has fallen from our head. Woe to us, for we have sinned. Because of this, our heart is sick;

> because of these, our eyes grow dim:
> because of Mount Zion, which lies deso-
> late and has jackals prowling in it. (Lam.
> 5:15–18)

Now hear the weeping of the exiled Hebrews from Judah:

> By the rivers of Babylon—there we sat
> down and wept when we remembered Zion.
> There we hung up our lyres on the poplar
> trees. . . . How can we sing the LORD's song
> on foreign soil? (Ps. 137:1–2, 4)

Like Adam and Eve, God's exiled people must have felt deeply homesick, grieving the loss of the ancient temple and their homeland and all the promises these places represented. Perhaps they wondered if their story as God's people was finally over. Perhaps they wondered if the torch Yahweh had given them to carry into the dark world—little *poiēmas* of his beauty—had been snuffed out for good.

Would they ever see the sunrise again? Or would this long, dark night last forever?

But prophets like Isaiah—the same prophets promising judgment, darkness, and desolation—also wove in words of hope and consolation. In exile's sunless night, God points to the light of a Son:

> The people walking in darkness have seen
> a great light; a light has dawned on those
> living in the land of darkness. . . . For a child
> will be born for us, a son will be given to us.
> (Isa. 9:2, 6)

This promised seed—this long-awaited Son—would accomplish the mission that Adam and Eve, and later Israel, had failed to fulfill. Where they were faithless, his delight would be in the fear of the Lord. Where they failed as a light to the nations, he would mirror God's glory to the world, "a banner for the peoples. The nations will look to him for guidance" (Isa. 11:10). When his light comes, "the LORD will shine over you, and his glory will appear over you. Nations will come to your light, and kings to your shining brightness" (Isa. 60:2–3).

Isaiah was active in Judah before they went into exile, and yet his words would likely have been read by the exiles weeping by the river in Babylon as well. The faithful would have clung to God's promise of a Son—this light dawning in the darkness—like Adam and Eve clung to the promise of the seed that would crush the serpent's head.

━━━━━━━

In the suffocating darkness of Mordor's caverns, Frodo and Sam come face-to-face with the giant, spiderlike creature Shelob, her menace bent on making a meal of two small hobbits. But just when all hope seems lost, Sam remembers the star-glass of Lothlórien, a gift from Lady Galadriel who promised it would be "a light when all other lights go out."[5] After finding the vial in his pocket, Frodo lifts it high in defiance along with his sword Sting. The hobbits watch in awe as its radiance causes the terrible creature to shrink away in fear. Galadriel's light would lead them all the way to the other side of the cave, back into the day.

Imagine God's people in exile: full of sorrow and yet waiting with hope, praying and longing for the dawn to pierce through all the dark. The faithful ones clinging to the promise of God's salvation just as Frodo clung to Galadriel's star-glass. When all the lights had gone out, when mighty Babylon and Assyria roared and mocked like Shelob, they held onto the hope of a promised Son who would one day come and, like a sunrise, "disperse the gloomy clouds of night, and death's dark shadows put to flight."[6]

This Advent, would you let the ache of your own exile, the dark shroud of your helplessness and sin, make Jesus's first advent, and his promised final advent, all the more glorious to you? Hold firm to your hope. Lift high the radiant light of the gospel. Watch in earnest for the sunrise breaking through and sing for joy at the sight of it!

RESPOND IN PRACTICE

Consider waking early tomorrow morning
or sometime this week to wait for the
sunrise. Choose a quiet place near your
home where you can see the long stretch
of the horizon. Arrive at least fifteen
minutes before the sun is forecasted to
come up—longer if you can. As you sit
waiting for the dawn to break, how do
you feel? Meditate on these words from
Luke 1: he comes "to give light to those
who sit in darkness and in the shadow of
death" (Luke 1:79 ESV).

He takes the thorns upon his head
His body pierced, his arms outstretched
Says "It is finished," and the sun went down
We laid his body in the ground . . .

But life oh life comes bursting forth
And paradise swings wide its doors!

from "We Wait for You"
by Caroline Cobb

Jesus as Exile in Reverse

Read John 1:1–18

> In the beginning was the Word, and the
> Word was with God, and the Word was
> God. . . . In him was life, and that life was
> the light of men. The light shines in the
> darkness, and yet the darkness did not
> overcome it. . . . The Word became flesh
> and dwelt among us. (John 1:1, 4–5, 14a)

Sit for a moment in the weightiness of the two exiles we have explored, first from Eden and then from the Promised Land. Remember the heartbreak Adam and Eve must have felt as they stumbled away from the garden. Listen for the groaning of the Hebrews, exiled in Babylon, as they mourned for their homeland and refused to sing the songs of Zion for their captors.

Stop. Feel the weight. Imagine again the midnight of exile, the dark before the dawn.

As the darkness of night stirs our longing for the sunrise, our sorrow over our own sin and the brokenness around us heightens our desire for the Savior. The black cloud draped over this period of judgment; the helplessness God's people felt to get back home to him—these shadows throw the bright beauty of Jesus's arrival into sharp relief.

The advent of Jesus should feel like a sunrise after a long, dark night or a flower budding from a stump in the middle of a burned-down forest. Like savoring the sweet taste of fruit after days and days of hunger. *At last! At last!*

In love, Jesus willingly leaves the abundant beauty and brilliance of heaven to make his home with us east of Eden. Once again, the Light shines in the darkness, the Presence bends low to breathe life into the dust.

Do you see it? Jesus is like exile thrown into reverse. His arrival marks the beginning of everything sad coming untrue.[7] *At last! At last!*

First, Jesus's advent reverses the withdrawal of God's presence. In Ezekiel 10–11, we saw Yahweh's glory cloud departing from both the temple and the city of Jerusalem. Because of their ongoing sin, God would no longer dwell among his beloved people or in their second Eden. But in Jesus, God's presence comes to us—not by filling up a physical temple or an Edenic garden but by inhabiting human form. When we could not find a way back home to God's presence, God's presence makes his way into our wilderness to "tabernacle" among us in his Son (John 1:14).[8] What an unexpected twist! "The presence of God, formerly contained in the Holy of Holies, has begun to burst forth into the world in the form of the incarnate God, Jesus Christ."[9]

Second, Jesus reverses God's judgment in exile. In the Old Testament, thorns are often emblematic of judgment and the consequences of sin. In Genesis 3:18, "thorns and thistles" are a primary symbol of the curse of sin. Over and over, the prophets image exile as a wilderness overgrown with thorns and briers (i.e., Isa. 7:23–24; Hosea 9:6). Is it a coincidence then that thorns and sharp nails would play so prominent a role in the death of Jesus? Picture the Roman soldiers twisting together the crown of thorns, shoving it roughly onto his bleeding head. See them holding him down on the wooden cross, hammering nails into his hands and feet. All of this was a visible symbol of an invisible spiritual reality: for our sake, he took the judgment of exile and bore our sins in his body (Gal. 3:13). And so we sing with joy each Christmas, "No more let sin or sorrows grow, nor thorns infest the ground! He comes to make His blessings flow far as the curse is found!"[10]

Darkness, yet another symbol of the curse, also plays a prominent role in the crucifixion story. As Jesus hung on the cross dying, "darkness came over the whole land . . . because the sun's light failed" (Luke 23:44–45). From noon to three p.m., the very time of day the sun always shines the brightest, Jerusalem is covered in thick darkness—almost as if the earth itself is grieving, cloaked in black funeral garb. The Light of the world is laid in the darkness of the tomb, taking on the death we deserve.

Finally, Jesus reverses our separation from God. Remember that in Genesis 3, God drives Adam and Eve out of his holy presence, stationing cherubim with flaming swords to guard the way back. Through the temple, Yahweh had been communicating both his desire to be with his people and their utter separation from him: "the common worshiper—even the average priest—would never stand in his presence. Only one man, once a year, entered the holy of holies, and he entered under the threat of death (Lev. 16:2). . . . God was once again with ʾĀdām, [Hebrew for "man"], but ʾĀdām was still separated from God."[11] But as Jesus breathes his last breath on the cross, something remarkable happens: the thick curtain separating the holy of holies from the outer courts tore from top to bottom (Matt. 27:51). And do you remember what image was sown into these curtains? Cherubim, symbolizing those fearful guardians of God's presence in Eden (2 Chron. 3:14). On our behalf, Jesus took the punishing blow of those swords ablaze, absorbing the punishment they were charged to administer and opening a "new and living way" back into God's presence (Heb. 10:20).[12] With these heavenly sentries no longer guarding the entry, the holy of holies now stood wide open.

Do you see it? With Jesus, *nothing* holds you back from leaving your exile behind and entering into the presence of a holy God. No curse, no curtain, no flaming sword or threat of death. If you are in Christ, nothing you have done or will do can separate you from God. In fact, it is appropriate to say that Jesus stands *beckoning* you, welcoming you into God's presence. Perhaps we can say even more: Jesus is the presence of God running out to find you lost in the darkness, picking you up, and carrying you across the threshold and into his kingdom of light.

When Adam and Eve bellow, *"We can't go back—there is no way,"* the voice of Jesus shouts, *"I am the Way!"* When we are lost in the thick darkness of exile, the Word of God speaks: *"Let there be light!"*

RESPOND IN PRAYER

Jesus, living Word of God, thank you for stepping into my exile and throwing it into reverse. You are the very presence of God, coming to dwell with us in human flesh. You took the curse of thorns and darkness I deserved and gave me life and light instead. Because you chose to separate yourself from your Father's heavenly home, even to the point of death on a cross, nothing can now separate me from his love (Phil. 2:8; Rom. 8:38–39). What a glorious and costly grace! Thank you, Jesus.

The King will rise to take his throne
And he will return to lead us home
To dry every tear and right every wrong
How long, O Lord?
How long, how long?

We wait, we wait for you.
Come with your light!

---

from "We Wait for You"
by Caroline Cobb

We All Long for Eden

Read 1 Peter 2:9–12

In a letter to his son, J. R. R. Tolkien famously wrote, "We all long for [Eden], and we are constantly glimpsing it: our whole nature at its best and least corrupted, its gentlest and most humane, is still soaked with the sense of 'exile.'"[13]

Do you feel it? We were created to be at home with God; but, as Advent reminds us, we know deep down that we are not. *At least not yet.* Jesus's first advent has indeed thrown our exile into reverse, but we still feel its effects.

Dare to look deep into the dark corners of your own heart. Watch the news. Drive around your town. Take stock of the things in our world that are not as they should be. Signs of our exile are all around us and rampant within us, too. Injustice, false gods, greed, empty religion, violence, disease, natural disasters, death. We know it when a child in our community faces leukemia. We feel it when a friend's secret addictions to alcohol or pornography or self-harm come to light. We see it in images of migrants gathering on overcrowded boats in the Mediterranean or at the border in Mexico. We live at a time when mass shootings in the West are no longer shocking, when we find ourselves idly wondering, *Why is the flag flown at half-mast today yet again?*, before we shrug it off and move along with our day.

And we feel our exile in smaller ways too. It's in the everyday shadows and "thorns" like wrinkles and weakening health, anxiety over our kids or our finances, in the quibble we have with a roommate or spouse, in the pang of loneliness we feel while scrolling social media, or even when we catch the flu.

In all this darkness—from the fleeting, everyday shadows to the deepest, blackest "dark night of the soul"—don't you long for the Light to come? Don't you ache for a new Eden, where every wrong will be made right and we will make our home with God forever?

At times, our sense of exile emerges not through a recognition of the darkness but through glimpsing its opposite in the light of the new Eden. If we are willing to look, we will find glimmers of this good light all around us. As poet Gerard Manley Hopkins wrote, "The world is charged with the grandeur of God. It will flame out, like shining from shook foil."[14] We see it shining as humans—reflecting God's image—work to preserve dignity, eradicate poverty, heal sickness, create beauty, and put the world right where it is broken. We see it in the church bringing salvation and hope. We catch glimpses of it in the warmth of true friendship, the redemptive beauty of a marriage restored, the suffering Christian who still chooses to praise God in her trial. We even see it in the flower growing wild and happy by the highway.

And yet, even these bright beams of kingdom light piercing through the darkness—as good as they are—only stir up an even deeper longing for the day when the shadows will be swallowed up altogether. One day, these glimmers of light will seem like darkness compared to the full light of new Eden's bright sun. As C. S. Lewis wrote, "They are not the thing itself; they are only the scent of a flower we have not found, the echo of a tune we have not heard, news from a country we have never visited."[15]

Lewis often used the German word *sehnsucht* to describe our inconsolable ache for "the thing itself," that pang of joy that awakens our desire for the transcendent beauty of the new Eden. As Lewis wrote in *Mere Christianity*, "If I find in myself desires which nothing in this world can satisfy, the only logical explanation is that I was made for another world."[16]

Scripture agrees; we belong to another world. Peter identifies us as "sojourners" and calls this period of waiting "the time of [our] exile" (1 Pet. 1:17; 2:9, 11 ESV). Our identity as "a chosen race, a royal priesthood, a holy nation, a people for [God's] own possession" (1 Pet. 2:9) inevitably results in dissonance; we will feel like exiles in a foreign land as we wait for the new creation to come in full. We are ambassadors of God's kingdom, citizens of a better country. We long for God's world like Adam and Eve longed for Eden, like the exiles pined for the Promised Land. As sons and daughters of God, we are not truly at home here. At least, not yet.

In Advent, we remember our identity as exiles and ask, *"How long, Oh Lord? When will you come to dry every tear and right every wrong? When will you come with your light and lead us home to your kingdom?"*

As we wait for that day, we link arms with Adam and Eve, the prophets, and the Old Testament exiles in Babylon and Assyria. Like them, we cling to God's promise of salvation and ache to see it fully realized. But we do so with a more vivid, concrete hope: a radiant, living, unchanging, imperishable, unconquerable hope anchored in the life, death, resurrection, and imminent return of our King and Savior, Jesus Christ (1 Pet. 1:3–5). A hope guaranteed by the Holy Spirit living inside us even now, sealing us as a people belonging to God (Eph. 1:13–14).

We do not despair in the darkness of our exile or our longing for home because the hope of Christ is as sure as the sunrise. Even now the dawn is breaking through, the firstfruits of that everlasting day.

RESPOND IN PRACTICE

Write your own prayer or poem
responding to God in your exile. Your
present circumstances or the darkness
you see around you might compel you to
write a lament, full of the ache of "how
long, O Lord?" Or perhaps you will praise
God for the glimmers of the new creation
you see—those beams of kingdom light
that make you long for "the thing itself."

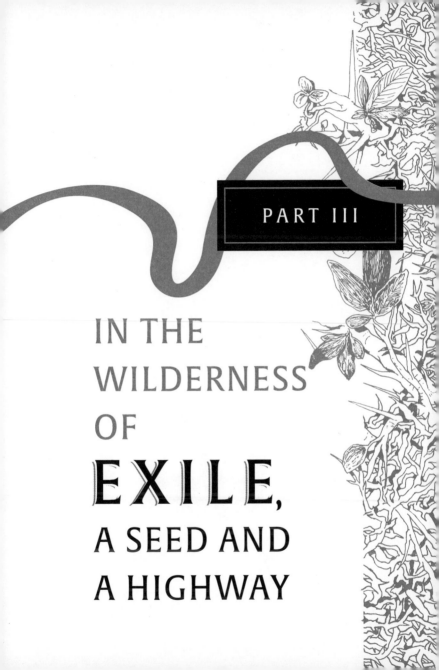

PART III

IN THE WILDERNESS OF EXILE, A SEED AND A HIGHWAY

Comfort, oh comfort
To every place that is scorched and dry
Comfort, speak comfort
To every darkness in need of the light

In the wilderness, the green of Eden
In the wasteland, the garden blooms
Up from the desert, springs a river
For he is making all things new

---

from "Comfort, Oh Comfort"
by Caroline Cobb

A Desolate Vineyard, A Better Vine

Read Isaiah 5:1–7; Isaiah 27:1–6

It takes at least three years to for a grape vine to begin producing fruit. The planting site must be carefully chosen, the vine planted at just the right depth and at just the right time of year, the soil cultivated to maintain an ideal pH level. Once growth begins, the vinedresser must follow specific trellis and pruning regiments. Diseases, mildew, invasive weeds, and pests must be vigilantly kept at bay.[1] In other words, cultivating a vineyard is not an amateur hobby. It is a tedious, costly, and time-consuming labor of love, reserved only for those who are passionately devoted.

The Old Testament often depicts ancient Israel as a vineyard, planted and cultivated by God himself. Moses sang, "You will bring them in and *plant* them on the mountain of your possession; LORD, you have prepared the place for your dwelling" (Exod. 15:17, emphasis added). Psalm 80 says, "You dug up a vine from Egypt; you drove out the nations and *planted* it. You cleared a place for it; it took root and filled the land" (vv. 8–9, emphasis added).

Isaiah 5 picks up this vineyard motif, describing the total care and devotion with which God has tended his people over their long history. *"What more could I have done for my vineyard than I did?"* he asks rhetorically (v. 4). He has done it all. And yet, at harvest time, the divine vinedresser discovers this tragic reality: his beloved vineyard has yielded only rotting, rancid grapes. In Hebrew, the word used here is literally "stink-fruit."[2] Bloodshed blooms where justice should be, a festering crop of broken relationships instead of righteous ones. On the outside, their religious rituals may have looked like good fruit, but they were rotten at the core, uprooted from Yahweh and his law. They had abandoned God, seeking nourishment and life elsewhere, and now they would be like "a waterless garden"—scorched, dry, and ready to be cast into the fire (Isa. 1:30).

> Therefore, as a tongue of fire consumes straw and as dry grass shrivels in the flame, so their roots will become like something rotten and their blossoms will blow away like dust, for they have rejected the instruction of the LORD. . . . Therefore the LORD's anger burned against his people. (Isa. 5:24–25)

Imagine a modern-day vinedresser discovering rotten grapes growing year over year, even after all his careful cultivation. At some point, he might choose to abandon the project but not without tremendous sorrow. We must keep this in mind as we read Isaiah's words. Holding *both* justified anger and tenderhearted sorrow, God will turn his face away from his beloved vineyard. He will remove its protective walls and hedges, allowing foreign enemies like Babylon and Assyria to trample it. "I will make it a wasteland. It will not be pruned or weeded; thorns and briers will grow up" (Isa. 5:6). Exile will transform his cherished vineyard people and their Edenic Promised Land into a desolate wilderness: scorched and dry, trampled and burned.

Picture a vineyard in California's famed Napa Valley, burned to ash, unattended, left alone to rot. *"What a tragedy,"* we would say as we drove past, hardly standing to look. How much more the sorrow of the vinedresser who has worked and tended these vines for so many years?

———

Israel's story could have ended right here. But, by God's grace, this is not the end. Isaiah points ahead to a day when God's vineyard will flourish once more:

> On that day sing about a desirable vineyard: I am the LORD, who watches over it to water it regularly. So that no one disturbs it, I watch over it night and day. I am not angry. If only there were thorns and briers for me to battle, I would trample them and burn them to the ground. . . . In the days to come, Jacob will take root. Israel will blossom and bloom and fill the whole world with fruit. (Isa. 27:2–4, 6)

> For the Lord will comfort Zion; he will comfort all her waste places, and he will make her wilderness like Eden, and her

> desert like the garden of the Lord. Joy and
> gladness will be found in her, thanksgiving
> and melodious song. (Isa. 51:3)

Do you hear it? In just a few chapters, God's tone toward his people has completely changed. His righteous anger, burning like fire toward his vineyard has become a tender word of comfort, and now his anger will burn against the "thorns and briers" instead. He will transform Zion's wilderness into the green of a new Eden, the barren wasteland of her own making into a garden. God is comforting his people in exile with a promise of undeserved restoration and flourishing.

But how? How do we account for this shift from well-earned judgment to unmerited delight? How can God grant a harvest of flourishing and joy when his people have continuously sown into idolatry and sin? In Isaiah's prophecy, we discover part of the answer. God will provide a new and better Vine:

> Then a shoot will grow from the stump of
> Jesse, and a branch from his roots will bear
> fruit. (Isa. 11:1)

When God's vineyard people could only produce rotten fruit, he promises a new and better branch who will bear fruit on their behalf. Grafted into this fruitful branch, God's people will take root, blossom, and bloom. Remember the "stink-fruit" and thorny wasteland of Isaiah 5? Now picture a flourishing vineyard tended and protected by God! He will cause it to grow like an Edenic garden until the whole earth is filled to bursting with its fruitful abundance!

Jesus is Isaiah's true and better Vine. He is the shoot growing up from the stump, the comfort and hope for the desolation of God's wayward vineyard people. And he is your hope and comfort as well. Hear him speak this invitation to you, even now: "I am the true vine, and my Father is the vinedresser. . . . I am the vine; you are the branches. Whoever abides in me and I in him, he it is that bears much fruit, for apart from me you can do nothing" (John 15:1, 5 ESV).

In Advent, we acknowledge our need for the true Vine. Without his coming, we would be a vineyard yielding only rotting grapes, a waterless garden. But Jesus *has* come! And he has promised to come again, bringing the fruitfulness of Eden into our wilderness. Even as you wait for the day you will abide in him forever, you are invited to abide now: grafted into his righteous life, yielding good fruit not because you are good in yourself but because you are united to the One who is.

RESPOND IN PRACTICE

Walk outside today and find a small plant, or purchase a houseplant at a nearby store. Break off a branch. Day by day, notice the way the disconnected branch withers away, especially compared to the branches that remain connected to the living plant. Let this image remind you of God's gracious invitation to abide in Christ, the Righteous Branch.

They will call him a Man of Sorrows
And like a seed, buried deep to rise again

In the wilderness, the green of Eden
In the wasteland, a garden blooms
Up from the desert, springs a river
For he is making everything new

from "Comfort, Oh Comfort"
by Caroline Cobb

Sown in weakness, raised in power
Sown in dust, death and dishonor
Raised immortal, never again to die
Death is swallowed up by life!

from "Wake Up"
by Caroline Cobb

The Seed of a New Creation

Read 1 Corinthians 15:20–23, 35–55

I have a little garden on the side of my house. It's embarrassingly weed-infested, and I have no idea what I'm doing. But, even still, seeds take root and grow. I marvel at it all the time. What kind of miracle causes a tiny, dormant seed to spring up into a tomato plant or a big bunch of leafy kale? And why exactly does the seed's burial in the dark tomb of the soil set such a miracle in motion? I don't pretend to know the answers, but I know this: without the seed's burial, there is no resurrection.

The exiles and prophets like Isaiah only glimpsed the Messianic hope we now see in full: Jesus is the promised "seed" of Adam and Eve arriving on the scene to crush the serpent's head at last (Gen. 3:15). Jesus is the shoot growing up from the stump, the Righteous Branch who will transform the thorny wilderness of exile into the green of the new Eden! But Jesus knew death must come first. His death would seed a garden of resurrection.

In the hours before his crucifixion, he told his disciples: "Truly I tell you, unless a grain of wheat falls to the ground and dies, it remains by itself. But if it dies, it produces much fruit" (John 12:24).

Sown into the earth, a seed must split open and "die" if new life is to take root. It's the only way. So Jesus would be laid down like a seed in the earth, buried deep. The Man of Sorrows would be "pierced because of our rebellion, crushed because of our iniquities; . . . cut off from the land of the living" (Isa. 53:5, 8). But as a seed rises miraculously from the soil, Jesus would also rise again—like the first green shoot sprouting up in my little garden, a sign of more growth to come. The Lord "will see his seed . . . and . . . justify many" (Isa. 53:10–11). Christ's sacrifice and death *will* bear fruit.

In Scripture, the seed metaphor maps onto the life of the believer through our union with Christ. According to Romans

6:3–11, the sin-sick "old self" we inherit from Adam is crucified with Christ on the cross and buried *with* him, just like a seed in a garden. But what happens next?

When a dormant seed is sown in the earth, it's embryo somehow "wakes up" and starts expanding, until at last it bursts through the seed coat and— eventually—through the soil. This is what happens to us when we are united to Jesus and what we are acting out in the sacrament of baptism: we are united *with* him in his death, only to be raised alive *with* him to "walk in newness of life" (Rom. 6:4). Resurrected with Jesus, we are no longer constrained by our hardened, sin-sick old self; it is cast aside and as powerless as the husk of a seed broken open. Through the Holy Spirit's awakening and regeneration, we are made into a "new creation" (2 Cor. 5:17). Re-created in Christ, we are as different as a dormant seed and a flower in full bloom.

And there is *more*! One day, we will be risen and re-created in *full*—both in soul *and* in body. Paul calls Jesus's bodily resurrection the "firstfruits" of a beautiful harvest yet to come. One day, Jesus will return, and our physical bodies—sown into the earth in weakness, dishonor, and perishable mortality—will be raised in imperishable glory (1 Cor. 15:20, 44).

Look and see it even now: a bright, colorful harvest of saints from every tribe and tongue bursting into the bloom of that final resurrection, like a field of wildflowers after the winter melts into spring. *At last! At last!*

———————

As you look at the landscape of your life, what do you see? Are there places that feel more like a burned-out forest than a flourishing garden? Perhaps your own sinful choices have left you feeling like a desolate wilderness. Perhaps the cares of the world have grown up slowly like weeds, choking out life and joy. Maybe someone else's sin against you, or even the brokenness of the world around you, seems to have burned all the beauty down to ash. We all have scorched and dry places in our stories, places where we begin to ask, "Can anything good grow up again in this wasteland?"

Take comfort, because it is precisely in these impossibly dry, desert places that God delights to make a garden grow. Jesus is the seed of the new creation, planted right in the middle of your exile and mine. He arrives not to seek out the best soil or to sow into only the most suitable plots of land. No, he arrives to bring beauty from the ashes and rivers in the wilderness! The Gospels show us that he had the most difficult time with the self-satisfied, righteous, religious types who saw themselves as already whole and fruitful, without any need for re-creation. Like hard soil, they were impermeable to the seed of good news. Do not be like them! Rather, let your "neediness" be like the furrows in a freshly-plowed field, like tilled soil open and ready to receive the sowing of resurrection life in Christ.[3]

This Advent, we remember the first arrival of Jesus, the seed of the new creation. But we also wait with hope for his second arrival. As we confess our need for him today, we also long for the day he will come to *fully* and *finally* transform our barrenness into the fruitful abundance of Eden.

RESPOND IN PRAYER

God, thank you for the words of comfort
you speak into my dry places, into all
the darkness in need of the light. You
see the landscape of my life and declare
that there is no place beyond Christ's
redemption and the Spirit's life-giving
power. In fact, your compassion compels
you all the more strongly to those places
where I feel most scorched and dry.

I look to you. I look to the God
who can make rivers spring up in the
desert and the green of Eden grow in
the wilderness. I set my hope on my
union with Christ. You are making me
into a new creation, and one day I will
dwell with you forever in the new Eden
to come—sown in weakness, raised to
imperishable glory.

Amen! Come, Lord Jesus, come!

Comfort, oh comfort
There is a highway through this dry land
We will call him the Man of Sorrows . . .

from "Comfort, Oh Comfort"
by Caroline Cobb

And the lamb that will come
His cross will be our doorway
And the red of his blood
It will wash us white

And daughters and sons
Rejoice in resurrection
And death swallowed up
In endless life!

from "The Passover Song"
by Caroline Cobb

The Highway in the New Exodus

Read Isaiah 43:16–25

Perhaps no image informed the collective identity of God's people like that of the exodus: their deliverance out of Egypt and the miraculous parting of the Red Sea. Every year, they would rehearse the exodus story by taking part in the Passover meal: eating food that reminded them of the bitterness of slavery and the sacrifice of the spotless lamb, hearing the story read over them once again. The Torah, the Psalms, the prophets—they all reference the exodus motif often, calling it to mind over and over through language, allusion, types, and patterns. At their core, the Hebrew people were an exodus people, ransomed *from* bondage and *to* God.

And so, it comes as no surprise that when Isaiah wants to give comfort and hope to God's people in exile, he points again and again to exodus imagery. Here is just a sampling:

> This is what the LORD says—who makes a way in the sea, and a path through raging water, who brings out the chariot and horse, the army and the mighty one together (they lie down, they do not rise again; they are extinguished, put out like a wick). (Isa. 43:16–17)

> Wasn't it you who dried up the sea, the waters of the great deep, who made the sea-bed into a road for the redeemed to pass over? (Isa. 51:10)

Once again, God's people find themselves in bondage to a terrible enemy. Once again, they are in desperate need of Yahweh's miraculous deliverance. Like the Hebrews shaking in their boots at the edge of the Red Sea, trapped between the oncoming Egyptian army and an impassable body of water, the exiles in Babylon and Assyria must have felt helplessly stuck. Their story seems to have come to a dead end. There is no way forward and no way back.

That is, unless God made a way. And in Isaiah, this is exactly what God promises to do. A *new exodus* is coming:

> Look, I am about to do something new;
> even now it is coming. Do you not see it?
> Indeed, *I will make a way in the wilderness.*
> (Isa. 43:19, emphasis added)

> A road will be there and a way; it will be called the Holy Way. The unclean will not travel on it, but it will be for the one who walks the path. Fools will not wander on it. . . . But the redeemed will walk on it, and the ransomed of the LORD will return and come to Zion with singing. (Isa. 35:8–10)

Isaiah promises a holy highway running through the desert wasteland, a road for God's ransomed people to follow out of their exile and all the way home to Zion. Remembering that Yahweh has made a way before, they can take comfort in his pledge to do it again. He *will* do it again!

But careful readers will notice a problem.

In his book *Exodus Old and New*, L. Michael Morales states the problem in plain language: "How can a second exodus make any more difference than the first? Though delivered physically out of Egyptian bondage, the hearts of God's people had remained in spiritual bondage."[4] Morales continues, "Israel's wayward heart . . . would not of itself be bent toward Yahweh, not even by the devastating agonies of exile."[5]

Isaiah draws attention to this problem when he says the highway out of exile would be a "Holy Way," off-limits to the "unclean." But if this is true, how will an unholy Israel, this wayward people who have wearied God with their many sins, ever walk this holy road? Prophets like Isaiah, Jeremiah, and Hosea have been adept at proving their uncleanliness, enumerating all the ways they have forsaken God over the years and how their sin had led them into exile in the first place. In and of themselves, God's people would never be holy or clean enough to access the highway Isaiah is describing.

Israel needed more than deliverance from literal captivity in Babylon and Assyria; they needed deliverance from the enslaving power of sin. They needed more than a physical road back to the city of Jerusalem; they needed a spiritual transformation, a return to God. They needed a deeper and better exodus, one that could remake them at the heart level, once and for all.

The arrival of Jesus initiates the *new* and *better* exodus Isaiah describes. Jesus comes as God's "Holy Highway" through the wilderness of our exile, his broken body providing "a new and living way" back into God's presence (Heb. 10:20). After eating the Passover meal with his disciples, Jesus takes up his cross as a new and better Passover lamb, paying our ransom price with his own blood and rescuing us forever from the plague of death (1 Pet. 1:19). Through Christ, the "unclean" are declared holy, his sinless life credited to our account (2 Cor. 5:21; Heb. 9:13–14). Jesus comes as a better Moses, leading us out of our slavery to sin and into a better Promised Land, the heavenly Zion where God makes his home among us forever. And one day, the powers of darkness and even death itself—the last enemy to be defeated—will be "swallowed up in victory," just as the Egyptians were swallowed up by the Red Sea (1 Cor. 15:26, 54)!

But why does all this matter during Advent? It matters because, at our core, we are still exodus people. There is perhaps no image more central to our collective identity as Christians than the cross and the empty tomb. Our miraculous salvation through Jesus—our exodus out of slavery under the curse of sin and death—defines our past, anchors us in our present exile, and animates our future hope. This is why we rehearse our redemption week after week at church: listening to the gospel story, singing songs of our deliverance, and taking part in the new Passover meal in the bread and wine of communion. When we do this, we are *looking back* on the new exodus Jesus initiated in his first advent. But we are also *looking forward*, staking our hope in his promise to bring us all the way home, until at last we are safe on Zion's golden shore.

RESPOND IN PRACTICE

Is there a river or some other body of water in your town? Is there a bridge that allows pedestrians or drivers to cross from one side to the other? Today or tomorrow, consider intentionally driving or walking over this bridge. As a secondary option, take a moment to imagine driving or walking this bridge in your mind's eye.

As you cross over the body of water, meditate on Jesus as the Way. He has made a way home to God; he is the highway leading us out of our exile. Ask yourself: What would it be like in your town if that bridge did not exist? Do you take it for granted? Consider how you might take for granted the access we have in Jesus. Respond in prayer.

Comfort, oh comfort
For the ransomed will return with a song
And with joy, we'll come into Zion
And all our sorrow, all our sighing will be gone

In the wilderness, the green of Eden
In the wasteland, the garden blooms
Up from the desert, springs a river
For he is making everything new

from "Comfort, Oh Comfort"
by Caroline Cobb

Pilgrims on the Way to Zion

Read Isaiah 35:1–10

For the last several years, summer has meant long road trips for our family of five: thirteen hours to the mountains of Colorado, fifteen hours to the Grand Canyon, seventeen hours to Disney World. Of course, no one particularly enjoys these long hours in the car, but we are spurred on by one important thing: the joy of our destination. The anticipation of the beauty and fun that await us gives us endurance to drive on and on. We all know that when we finally get there, we will look back on the long journey and say, *"Worth it!"*

In the same way, the prophet Isaiah comforts the exiles by giving them a grand vision of their final destination. *"Look!"*

he says, *"your future is in the new Eden, a city filled with unending joy!"*

> The ransomed of the LORD will return and come to Zion with singing, crowned with unending joy. Joy and gladness will overtake them, and sorrow and sighing will flee. (Isa. 35:10)

> For I will create new heavens and a new earth; . . . I will rejoice in Jerusalem and be glad in my people. The sound of weeping and crying will no longer be heard in her. . . . They will not do what is evil or destroy on my entire holy mountain. (Isa. 65:17–19, 25)

The exiles in Babylon and Assyria longed for their homeland, and they surely clung to these promises from Isaiah. But they were *stuck*. Strong enemies and a vast wilderness barred their way back. Even as they waited with hope for Isaiah's vision to become reality, they also knew they were not yet on the road.

But the arrival of Jesus means our experience is different. We need not think of ourselves as stuck because, through

Jesus, God has *already* made a way. His life, death, and resurrection have paved the promised highway through the wilderness, and we are already *en route*! We are more than just exiles far from home; we are pilgrims on the move. The glorious vision of our future destination strengthens our tired feet and feeble knees, urges us forward when the path seems long, and infuses the often difficult journey with deep hope. Even more, God does not leave us to walk alone. He is beside us and within us through his Spirit, promising to shepherd and sustain us in every step—until the end.

One day, we will come into Zion, that heavenly garden city even better than Eden.[6] All sorrow and sighing, death and decay will be gone forever. Instead of the thornbush, a garden will bloom, and mighty trees will grow tall (Isa. 55:13). Instead of being surrounded by the longing groans of the exiles hanging up their harps, we will be overwhelmed by a joyful anthem of praise, pouring out from the lips of countless saints and angels. And God himself will bend close to tenderly wipe your tears and mine (Isa. 25:8; Rev. 7:17). His presence makes the heavenly city beautiful. If you are in Christ, you are already on the path winding toward this glorious destination, moving ever closer day by day.

Our neighborhood holds a Fourth of July parade every year. There is singing and dancing, cheering and waving, candy throwing and fun with friends. Perhaps you can picture a similar parade in your neighborhood or town. When I read passages like Isaiah 35, I can't help but picture a parade like our Fourth of July parade but *far more* beautiful and joyous! Isaiah's word picture speaks of the reversal of the curse of exile: somehow this pilgrim procession transforms the wilderness into an Edenic garden and the dry land into gushing springs![7]

Can you imagine it even now? Picture a barren desert, scorched by the sun. But there—just up over the horizon—you see a crowd advancing. Is that singing you hear? Wait, are they dancing? Do you see the wildflowers and streams springing up in their footsteps? Ransomed child of God, can you picture yourself among them?

Look around you; every color, ethnicity, language, and age are represented in this hope-filled march. As Spirit-filled citizens of heaven, we are throwing not candy but the seeds of resurrection. As the beloved of God, we are celebrating not a national holiday but our freedom and adoption as sons and daughters of the King. And all along the way, we are spreading the fragrance of Christ, bringing new life to barren places, and inviting others to join us in our joyful parade (2 Cor. 2:14–16).

God is making all things new, Christ is leading us in triumphal procession, and the Spirit is energizing our every step. If you are in Jesus, you are a pilgrim making your way to a heavenly new Jerusalem, where God will make his home with you forever and you will see him face-to-face.

We know that when we arrive in Zion at last, we will look back on the long journey and heartily declare, *"Worth it!"* The apostle Paul says it this way: "For our momentary light affliction is producing for us an absolutely incomparable eternal weight of glory. So we do not focus on what is seen, but on what is unseen" (2 Cor. 4:17–18).

Advent invites you to remember and rehearse your pilgrim identity. Today, it bids you to practice the discipline of journeying with anticipation, eyes focused on an unseen, eternal destination beyond compare, and—even more!—on the glorious God who makes his home there. Surely, he is worth it all.

RESPOND IN PRAYER (INSPIRED BY PSALM 84)

Oh Lord, how lovely is your dwelling place! A day in your presence is better than a thousand elsewhere. My soul longs—it even faints—for you. The living God! Set my feet on this pilgrim way and fix my eyes on eternity, forsaking all detours and distractions.

God, thank you for the fellow pilgrims I am marching alongside [take a moment here to list specific names—church community, friends, mentors, leaders]. May we go from strength to strength even as we walk through this wilderness. With each footstep, would you somehow use us to turn the valley of tears into springs of fresh water and barren places into flourishing gardens. Amen.

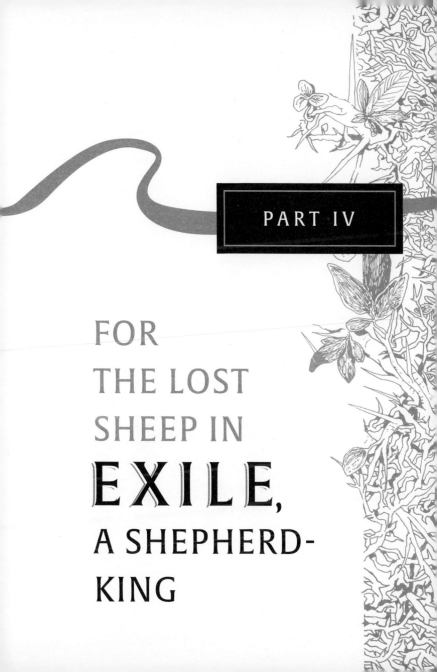

PART IV

FOR
THE LOST
SHEEP IN
EXILE,
A SHEPHERD-
KING

Oh Righteous Branch from Jesse's root
Please come and bring your kingdom
The lion dwelling with the lamb
Bring peace and life and freedom

Oh Son of David come to rule
And reign in us forever
Come write your law upon our hearts
And keep us like a shepherd

Hallelujah, Jesus we wait for you
Hallelujah, Jesus come soon, come soon

---

from "Oh Righteous Branch"
by Caroline Cobb

Come, Son of David!

Read 2 Samuel 7:1–16; Psalm 89:1–4, 35–41

David was out tending his family's sheep when he received a message from his father Jesse: "Come home quickly, son. An important visitor wants to meet you." Soon after, Samuel the prophet was anointing him with oil. David felt it run warm down his head and into his beard. The youngest son of Jesse, this lowly shepherd, had been chosen as king of Israel.

The act of anointing "symbolized the outpouring of God's Spirit in empowerment for new office."[1] Although far from perfect, David would become emblematic for Israel: the standard-bearer for a godly, faithful king. Under his leadership, the nation experienced a golden age marked by victory over enemies, peace on all sides, a flourishing kingdom full of justice, and unhindered covenant fellowship with Yahweh.

In 2 Samuel 7, God makes David an astonishing promise:

> "I took you from the pasture, from tending the flock, to be ruler over my people Israel. . . . I will raise up after you your descendant, who will come from your body, and I will establish his kingdom. He is the one who will build a house for my name, and I will establish the throne of his kingdom *forever.*"
> (2 Sam. 7:8, 12–13, emphasis added)

According to Old Testament scholar Sandra Richter, this promise will become "the taproot of the messianic hope," looming large in the collective imagination of God's people.[2] From this point forward, they lived in anticipation of this promised Son of David, an "anointed One" who would somehow shepherd God's flock not merely for a season but forever. With every new king, I imagine they wondered: *Could this be the One?*

―――――

But king after king fell short of David's standard. In just two generations, civil war split the nation in two. With few exceptions, the kings of both the northern and southern kingdoms strayed further and further from God's ways. And under these shepherds, the people strayed too. Listen to God's harsh words of judgment for the leaders of this time: "You have scattered my flock and have driven them away, and you have not attended to them. Behold, I will attend to you for your evil deeds" (Jer. 23:2 ESV). The prophet Zechariah employs a horrifyingly violent image: shepherds devouring their fattest sheep—even ripping off their hooves—and abandoning the weak ones to die (Zech. 11:16–17).

By the time of the exile, David's golden age was a distant memory. Enemies gathered at the gates, injustice was everywhere, and the people had broken covenant too many times to count. Without a shepherd king like David, God's people became easy prey for prowling enemies like Babylon and Assyria.

On other side of exile, God's people must have asked, *"What about God's promise to David? The one our parents and teachers told us about? Oh, where is the Son of David God said would rule forever?"* Surely, their longing felt more acute than ever. They *ached* for a king anointed by God and empowered by his Spirit to fight for them. They *yearned* for a shepherd like David to come and carry them home. *"Oh God, will you keep your promise? Have you forgotten?"*

Psalm 89 gives voice to these honest questions. The psalmist spends the first two-thirds of his prayer recounting God's covenant with David, but in the final third he is lamenting what looks like God's failure to follow through. He is *begging* the Lord to reconcile the promise of David's perpetual kingdom with the utter desolation of exile he sees all around him:

> The LORD said, "I have made a covenant with my chosen one; I have sworn an oath to David my servant: 'I will establish your offspring forever and build up your throne for all generations.'" . . . But you have spurned and rejected him; you have become enraged with your anointed. You have repudiated the covenant with your servant; you have completely dishonored his crown. (Ps. 89:3–4, 38–39)

You can almost hear the psalmist's heartbreak and confusion: *"Oh God, this just does not add up! What will you do now?"*

Prophets like Isaiah and Jeremiah speak words of comfort into these honest questions. To the shepherdless exiles who could not reconcile their circumstances with the promises of God, the prophets make this proclamation: the Messiah, the anointed King you long for, *is* coming!

Isaiah says, "Then a shoot will grow from the stump of Jesse, and a branch from his roots will bear fruit" (Isa. 11:1). God elaborates through Jeremiah:

> "I will gather the remnant of my flock from
> all the lands where I have banished them,
> and I will return them to their grazing land.
> . . . I will raise up a Righteous Branch for
> David. He will reign wisely as king and
> administer justice and righteousness in the
> land. . . . This is the name he will be called:
> The LORD Is Our Righteousness." (Jer.
> 23:3, 5–6)

If you read carefully here, you will notice the promised King comes not from the root of *David* but from that of his father *Jesse*.[3] In other words, God's anointed One is not merely a physical son of David but a *new David* far better than the first.[4]

Jesus is the new and better David! Through Jesus the good Shepherd, the same mighty arm that scattered the people into exile would now tenderly gather up his lost sheep, drawing them close to his chest: "He gathers the lambs in his arms and carries them in the fold of his garment" (Isa. 40:11). Jesus will build a house for God's name, gathering up the lost sheep from every nation and inviting them inside. And he will reign as King over this house forever.

Like the Old Testament exiles, we long for good and just shepherds too. Instead, we often find bosses who overwork and underpay, politicians politicking rather than serving, authorities failing to protect the vulnerable. And one glance at the headlines will tell you the church is not immune: false teachers twisting the truth to prey on the weak, leaders tending their brand rather than God's flock, "wolves in sheep's clothing" being exposed day after day. Of course, there are many faithful Christian leaders, but these will be the first to acknowledge the ways they fall short. Advent helps us remember that we have a better King, a good Shepherd anointed to lay down his life for God's sheep (John 10:11). In Advent, we ache for his kingdom to come in full.

RESPOND IN PRAYER

Jesus, Son of David, no earthly king, political party, or leader—even in your church—will ever measure up to you. You are our good Shepherd and God's anointed King. Without you, we are lost and vulnerable sheep—easy prey for the enemy. This Advent, we watch and wait for the day you will gather up your sheep and consummate your reign. Come, Son of David. Come, good Shepherd. Jesus, we wait for you. Amen.

Messiah, come, your Spirit give
Turn stony hearts to flesh
Redeem us from captivity
The power of sin and death

At last, at last the morning comes
With healing in its wings
We'll leap like calves loosed from their stalls
For you have done great things!

From "Oh Righteous Branch"
by Caroline Cobb

Hosanna on the Horizon

Read Isaiah 62:6–12; Matthew 20:25–28

The Old Testament story ends without any real resolution. In 539 BC, Persia defeats Babylon, and King Cyrus allows the exiled Jews there to return home. A small band makes their way back to the Promised Land, rebuilding the walls around Jerusalem and reconstructing the temple. And yet, their experience falls far short of true restoration. God's people may have physically come home, but they still felt the ache of exile and longed for the arrival of their King.

Ezra tells us that when the elders and priests who remembered the glory of the first temple witnessed the new one being built, they started *weeping*. The sound of their grief could not be distinguished from the shouts of joy coming from the younger generation (Ezra 3:10–13). The temple, the city, the land—it just wasn't the same, and the elders knew it. Even more, though many exiles had returned home, Israel as a whole was still scattered abroad. The remnant who had returned had no king or land of their own. After exile, they lived in an almost constant state of foreign occupation—first under Persia, then Greece, then Rome.

God's people were living in tension between joy at being "home" and grief over what God had not yet restored. Their story felt incomplete, the faithful still waiting for the climactic ending—the promised King arriving to bring Israel back to glory. Isaiah uses the image of a watchman set on Jerusalem's walls, straining his eyes day and night as he watches for God to keep his promises.

In Advent, we take up our post as watchmen as well. This season reminds us that our story is not yet complete. Like the Israelites after exile, we scan the horizon for signs of our coming King.

By the time of Jesus's birth in the first century, the Jews had a diverse understanding of how to live like "watchmen on the walls." The Essenes withdrew to cloistered communities;

the Pharisees escalated strictness about laws and separation; the Zealots often tried to hasten revolution through violence. But these groups had one thing in common: most expected a kingly Messiah to come suddenly and with great military might, sweeping away the pagan oppressors and raising Israel back to power.[5]

Jesus, God's King and Messiah, defies these expectations. Instead of having a royal birth in a palace, our King is born quietly to poor parents and laid in a feeding trough. Instead of commandeering us to care for his every need, he bends low as a servant to wash our feet. Instead of throwing off the oppression of earthly powers like Rome, he comes to liberate us from a more pressing enemy and from the cosmic powers of sin and death. Throughout his life, he wields not an iron fist but a compassionate touch for the unclean leper, the bleeding woman clinging to his robes, the blind beggar on the roadside calling out, "Have mercy on me, Son of David!" (Matt. 8:2–4; Matt 9:20–22; Mark 10:46–52).

To Simon Peter the zealot, Jesus says, "Put your sword away!" (John 18:11). To the law-keeping scribes and Pharisees, he says, "Let the one who has never sinned throw the first stone!" (John 8:7 NLT). To the ones who would withdraw from the Gentiles, Jesus says, "Go, therefore, and make disciples of all nations" (Matt. 28:19).

As king, Jesus refuses to pile impossible laws higher and higher like the religious leaders tended to do. Instead, he follows God's laws perfectly in our place (Matt. 5:17–18; Rom. 5:18–19; 8:3–4). Then, he writes them on our hearts through his Spirit, knowing we could never keep them in our own power (Jer. 31:33; Ezek. 36:26–27).

During his last week of life, we see Jesus ride into Jerusalem like a king (John 12:12–16). This scene fulfills Zechariah's prophecy: "Rejoice greatly, Daughter Zion! Shout in triumph, Daughter Jerusalem! Look, your King is coming to you; he is righteous and victorious, humble and riding on a donkey" (Zech. 9:9). The Jewish people lining the streets were feverish with hopeful expectation, throwing down palm branches and shouting, "Hosanna to the Son of David!" (Matt. 21:9) The word *hosanna* means "save us!"

In this moment, the metaphorical watchmen on the walls are wide-eyed and pointing excitedly in Jesus's direction: *"It's the King at last! Here he comes! Salvation is here!"* But again, most thought God's salvation would look like an overthrow of Rome. Imagine their disappointment when, just a few days later, that same Jesus hung dying on a Roman cross. The sign above him read, "THIS IS JESUS, THE KING OF THE JEWS" (Matt. 27:37).

Most of God's people did not have a category for a suffering king, only a conquering one. And yet, Jesus's suffering is *exactly* the means God would use to save us. When the people lining the streets cried "Hosanna!," he answered by taking up the cross.

And just as King Jesus defied expectations, so did his kingdom. When the mother of two of his disciples asked if her sons could rule beside him, one sitting on the left and one on the right, Jesus flips the traditional understanding of power on its head:

> You know that the rulers of the Gentiles lord it over them, and those in high positions act as tyrants over them. It must not be like that among you. On the contrary, whoever wants to become great among you must be your servant, and whoever wants to be first among you must be your slave; just as the Son of Man did not come to be served, but to serve, and to give his life as a ransom for many. (Matt. 20:24–28)

Jesus would also say the kingdom of heaven would not come all at once but small and slowly like a mustard seed or a bit of leaven in dough (Matt. 13:33–35). Like the planting of a seed or the sprinkling of yeast, Jesus's arrival set something in motion that cannot be stopped. His kingdom is *already* here, expanding day by day. And yet Advent reminds us that we live in the space between his kingdom's inauguration and inevitable consummation. So we take up our posts as watchmen on the walls, looking for our King to return and finish what he has started.

On that day every knee will bow, either willingly or unwillingly. For those who refuse to submit to King Jesus in this life, the last day will be terrible. But God's people will meet it with joy. We will leap like cooped-up calves finally loosed from their stalls (Mal. 4:2)! And we will sing together, "he has done great things" (Ps. 126:3)!

RESPOND IN PRACTICE

Take a moment to listen twice through the hymn "O Come, O Come Emmanuel" or my song "Oh Righteous Branch." Set the lyrics in front of you. The first time through, quietly meditate on the words. The second time you listen, sing along. As you sing, make these words your prayer to King Jesus, stirring up your anticipation for his arrival.

Eternal God, there at the beginning
Stepping into time, into the world
All for love, the infinite descending
To kick inside the womb of a girl

A king is born, far from any palace
Bending low to serve instead
Majesty, he's given up his status
Robed in the weakness of the flesh

Unto us a child is born
Heaven coming down to earth
Joy to all the weary world
The human soul will feel its worth

Joy to the world! Good, good news!
Oh come let us adore him!
Joy to the world! It's breaking through!
He's come and he will come again!

---

from "Joy (As Far As The Curse is Found)"
by Caroline Cobb

Majesty, Bending Low in Love

Read Isaiah 6:1–5; Philippians 2:5–11

In A. W. Tozer's famous treatise on the attributes of God, *The Knowledge of the Holy*, he observes: "Until [a person] sees a vision of God high and lifted up, there will be no woe and no burden. Low views of God destroy the gospel for all who hold them."[6]

Here, Tozer is using the language of Isaiah 6: "I saw the Lord sitting upon a throne, high and lifted up; and the train of his robe filled the temple" (Isa. 6:1 ESV).

Put yourself in Isaiah's shoes for a moment. Listen to the thundering voices of the seraphim declaring "Holy, holy,

holy is the LORD of hosts; the whole earth is full of his glory!" (Isa. 6:3 ESV). Imagine the room filling with smoke. Feel the foundations of the temple shaking beneath your feet. You are shaking too, trembling and terrified at this overwhelming vision of our holy God, reigning from his heavenly throne. How would you respond?

Isaiah's response would—and should—be our natural response as well: "Woe is me for I am ruined because I am a man of unclean lips and live among a people of unclean lips, and because my eyes have seen the King, the LORD of Armies" (Isa. 6:5).

This is the woe and burden to which Tozer is referring. In order to appreciate the beauty of the gospel, we must feel the weight of our sin and our helplessness as sinners before a holy God.

In a sense, Advent is a season set aside for just this experience. During Advent, we acknowledge the vast separation between us and God in order to set the table for the astonishing goodness of the Christmas-gospel: Jesus, the King of heaven, has been sent to close the distance.

Take a moment to consider Tozer's statement again in light of the incarnation. How much more would we treasure the good news that Jesus came as a human infant if we saw him high and lifted up? Just how low did our Savior have to descend to redeem us? What abundant riches did he lay aside to make his home with bankrupt sinners like us? What overflowing compassion would compel the Light of the world to be born into the darkness of our exile? What kind of love would compel the King of kings to stoop this far and from such a height?

One by one, meditate on these profound realities:

Jesus, the eternal Word, knowing no end or beginning . . .

> *Embracing the constraints of creation: time,
> space, and even death itself.*

Jesus, the infinite, omnipresent, limitless Son of God . . .

> *Kicking in the cramped womb of an average,
> small-town teenage girl.*

Jesus, the incomprehensible, unseen, transcendent . . .

> *Born in human form that we might know
> what God is like. Touch him, see him, smell
> him, hear his voice. So human.*

Jesus, the sovereign, majestic, omniscient King of heaven . . .

"Emptied himself by assuming the form of a servant, taking on the likeness of humanity" (Phi. 2:7).

Jesus, the perfectly holy one, spotless, dwelling in unapproachable light . . .

Descending into our darkness, bearing our sin and sorrow, dying the death we deserve, coming to make his blessings flow as far as the curse is found.

How low then did King Jesus descend to be with us in our exile? To empathize with our suffering? To die for us and redeem us? Our minds and hearts cannot begin to fathom.

As we consider these truths, the only proper response is *worship*. Come bow down before him with the wise men! Prepare to praise him with songs of joy alongside the angels! Let the weary world rejoice that he bent this low, coming into our exile to make his blessings flow as far as the curse is found! Let the human soul feel it's worth—that God would pay such a price to bring us home to him.

Oh, come let us adore him, even as we wait for him to come again.

RESPOND IN PRACTICE

Go back to the five truths about Jesus listed in the reflection today (Jesus, the . . .), and the corresponding way Jesus "emptied himself" in his incarnation. Meditate on these beautiful gospel realities again, but this time use them as prompts for prayer, worship, and confession. Pause at each one and respond in your own words. Do you see Christ as high and lifted up? Do you feel woe and burden like Isaiah? Do you marvel at how low he descended to be with us? Consider praying aloud, writing your prayer out, or even getting into a group and using these words in a call-and-response format. (Leader: "Jesus, the ____." Together, the people answer with Jesus's action.)

Pave every road with repentance
Bring the proud heart low
Let the humble heart sing
Break down all your walls, your defenses
Swing wide your gates
For the coming of the King!

One day we'll all hear the trumpet
He will return with reckoning
And I'll follow my King into glory
Who here is coming with me?
Who here is coming with me?

Get up! Get ready!
Get up! Get ready for the King to come!

----

from "Pave Every Road"
by Caroline Cobb

Pave Every Road with Repentance

Read Isaiah 40:1–11; Matthew 3:1–3

What is the purpose of the Advent season? If we are honest, most of us treat the four weeks leading up to December 25 almost like a pre-Christmas warm-up. December means making shopping lists for friends and family, taking advantage of winter sales, listening to Bing Crosby, attending holiday parties, and drinking Starbucks gingerbread lattes. For most of us, this season is about being busy with merry preparation. But John the Baptist, herald of the Messiah, tells us a different story of how to make ready in the days leading up to Christ's arrival. According to John, we prepare through *repentance*. Repentance paves the way for the King.

Imagine yourself as a first-century Jew in Jerusalem. For more than four hundred long years, no prophet has spoken. There has been no word from God, no spiritual movement. About thirty years ago, you heard rumors of some shepherds getting excited about a baby born nearby, but you haven't heard much since. So you keep the feasts, listen to the Torah's stories, attend temple every week, and try your best to keep an eye out for the promised Messiah. But he has been so long in coming, and life holds so many other, more pressing concerns.

Suddenly, you hear of a prophet preaching down by the Jordan River. A voice crying out in the wilderness, shattering the silence. Out of curiosity, you make your way out to see what all the hubbub is about, only to hear the first prophetic word in five generations: "Repent, because the kingdom of heaven has come near!" (Matt. 3:2).

Like the prophets who had come before him, John did not mince words about sin and the need for forgiveness. He reserved his harshest condemnation for the religious leaders, calling them a "brood of vipers" and telling them being a part of Abraham's physical family tree would not save them from the judgment to come, only bearing fruit in keeping with repentance (Matt. 3:7–9). "The ax is already at the root of the trees," he told them. "Therefore, every tree that doesn't produce good fruit will be cut down and thrown into the fire" (Matt. 3:10). To ensure they do not mistake him for the Messiah, and to make the reason for his urgency clear, he says,

> I baptize you with water for repentance, but the one who is coming after me is more powerful than I. I am not worthy to remove his sandals. He himself will baptize you with the Holy Spirit and fire. His winnowing shovel is in his hand, and he will clear his threshing floor and gather his wheat into the barn. But the chaff he will burn with fire that never goes out. (Matt. 3:11–12)

John the Baptist's warnings preclude indifference; there could be no shrugging off John's words. The "one who is coming" is just around the bend. So, many came forward to acknowledge their sin, stepping into the Jordan to repent and be baptized. They were making themselves ready for the advent of the Messiah.

At last, the long-awaited King is coming! This Advent, John has been sent to tip us off, to goad us out of a sleepy religion that presumes on God and wake us up to the reality of the Christ's immanent arrival. Indifference is not an option. Action *must* be taken. How will we make ready?

The Gospels tell us that John the Baptist is the fulfillment of the prophet Isaiah's promise from so many years before (John 1:23):

> Prepare the way of the LORD in the wilderness; make a straight highway for our God in the desert. Every valley will be lifted up, and every mountain and hill will be leveled; the uneven ground will become smooth and the rough places, a plain. And the glory of the LORD will appear, and all humanity together will see it, for the mouth of the LORD has spoken. (Isa. 40:3–5)

In the ancient Near East, monarchs, foreign dignitaries, and "gods" who wanted to visit neighboring cities would often travel on "highways" constructed specifically for their procession.[7] Servants would go ahead of them—clearing out rocks and debris, filling in potholes, removing every obstacle. They were making rough terrain smooth for their king, ensuring that nothing would stand in the way of his arrival.[8] The imagery in Isaiah 40 draws on this tradition but calls even the mountains to bow low and the valleys to rise. Here we see that this King of Isaiah 40 is no ordinary, earthly king. The King of kings, the Lord of heaven and earth is on his way. The one who will baptize with fire and the Holy Spirit is planning to pay us a visit.

Advent is a yearly clarion call to "prepare the way of the Lord." It is an invitation to bring our proud egos low, to root out the rocks and weeds blocking the highway to our hearts, to acknowledge our sin and lower our defenses. If we are to make ready for King Jesus, we must heed John the Baptist's exhortation. The hurry and excess of the holiday season often distract us from the truth of our exile, numbing us to the sufferings and sins we harbor deep down and to the brokenness around us. But Advent summons us to face the reality of these things head-on.

To be clear, this is not a call to endless penance or a hopeless, wallowing self-hatred. This aspect of Advent is not an end to itself but a *primer*. We take an honest assessment of our sin and the sin around us in order to awaken anticipation for the Savior we so desperately need. The "bad news" John the Baptist preached—that we are sinners in need of repentance and forgiveness—sweetens the good news he also proclaimed: "Look, the Lamb of God, who takes away the sin of the world!" (John 1:29) Again, Advent magnifies the glorious beauty of Christmas.

With this in mind, how will you make ready for the King? What would it mean for you to swing wide your gates for his coming?

What if, in the four weeks leading up to December 25, we focused a little less on preparing ourselves for Christmas through merry making and cookie baking, and instead prepared ourselves primarily through repentance? What if we made ready for the coming of King Jesus not by taking an inventory of gifts to buy, parties to attend, and traditions to keep, but by "taking a fearless inventory of the darkness: the darkness without and the darkness within?"[9]

Again, the invitation of Advent is not to be a sullen spoilsport. Please don't feel the need to fast from gingerbread lattes or wear a John-the-Baptist-style camel-hair suit to the holiday party. But *do* repent. Advent repentance is not a Christmas killjoy. Rather, it paves the way for a sweeter, more expansive joy—better than parties, traditions, or gifts could ever provide.

Hear John the Baptist's words to you even now: "Repent! The King is coming!" Are you ready?

RESPOND IN PRAYER

God, let me hear the voice in the wilderness crying, "Repent! Prepare the way of the Lord." I confess my pride and lower my defenses. I confess being caught up in the hurry and excess of this season. Humble me and sober me today, I pray. Give me an urgency to get ready! Help me swing wide my gates, longing for the coming of the King. Amen.

(Spend a few moments taking inventory of the brokenness without and within. Linger until you feel the palpable need for a Savior. Then, run to the gospel.)

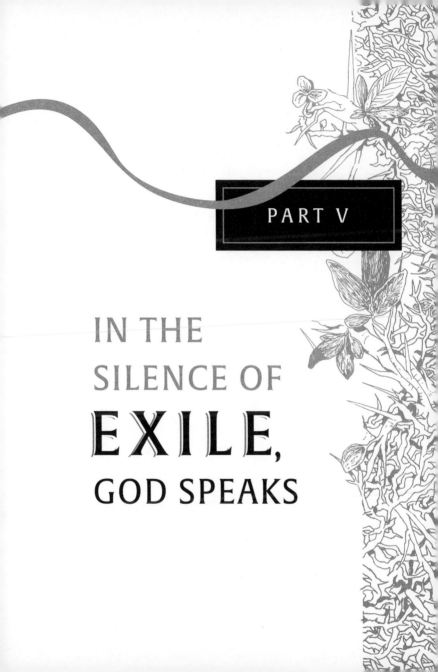

PART V

IN THE
SILENCE OF
EXILE,
GOD SPEAKS

In a tiny town
In the dark of night
From a run-down stable
Came a baby's cry

He was wrapped in rags
And his parents were poor
But the baby in the manger
Was Christ the Lord

Hallelujah! Christ is born!
Hallelujah! The Savior of the world!
This is the one we've waited for
Hallelujah! Hallejuah!
Christ is born!

---

from "Hallelujah, Christ is Born"
by Caroline Cobb

The Cosmic Word in Human Flesh

Read Luke 2:1–7

This Advent devotional invites you to consider some very "cosmic" biblical concepts: the problem of sin and our need for salvation, the Light stepping into our darkness, the Davidic King, the Righteous Branch, the ancient idea of the Messiah. But, as beautiful and biblical as these ideas are, there is a danger of becoming a bit too "cosmic" about Advent and Christmas. We can start living with our heads in a cloud of abstractions and poetic metaphors, engaging with the season as an academic pursuit or aesthetic experience but never understanding what it has to do with our ordinary, messy lives.

If we let it, the birth story of Jesus can bring us back down to earth. Our abstract theology around the "seed of the new Eden" and "the Righteous Branch" gets distilled into flesh and blood. In the dirty stable of Bethlehem, God is no longer a concept to study from a safe distance but a relational being who is willing to be born right into our mess. Compared to the prophets' dramatic promises of a mighty Davidic King, the birth of Jesus seems almost too quiet and insignificant, too lowly and human. But this is the beautiful miracle of Christmas: the cosmic entering the gritty human story, the prophets' exalted, anointed King walking around on the dusty streets of our real world.

Imagine being in the midst of a census, everyone traveling to their ancestral cities to be counted. It is all chaos and crowds, all noise and odor and dust, roads clogged with people and animals jockeying for a place to stay until they can get back home. Imagine a road-worn Joseph weaving through the congested streets, leading his very-pregnant fiancée to a back-alley cattle stall. *"This will have to do,"* Joseph says wearily as he prepares a makeshift bed out of hay for Mary.

Now envision Mary laboring there in the straw, all alone in her pain but for Joseph. Wincing with each contraction, straining to push, a brow beaded with sweat, tears on cheeks, a surge of blood and amniotic fluid and—at last!—a baby. Joseph and Mary shushed the crying infant, cleaning him and wrapping him tight in swaddling rags, feeding him, then laying him down to sleep in a feeding trough meant for livestock.

A human birth is always messy and without pretension, humbling and—well, *humanizing*. If you have ever been in the room with a woman in labor or witnessed the reality of childbirth, you know this to be true. In the moments and days after my oldest was born, I kept thinking, *This is absolutely nothing like the movies!* But Jesus's birth seems to be even messier than most. Born in a dirty stable to a simple carpenter and his fiancée, the cries of pain, the smell of blood and sweat and cattle . . . this birth seems particularly lowly and crude. We might even say it was dishonorable, ignoble, shameful.

Oh that Jesus would be born at all! And in this particular way?

We can also infer that the family God chose for Jesus was likely not rich or even middle-class, but poor. Later, when Mary and Joseph brought their baby to the temple to present him to the Lord, they offered up a pair of birds. According to Leviticus 10, those who offered turtledoves or pigeons would only do so because they could not afford a proper lamb. As Bible teacher Christine Gordon writes, "The One who authored history, marked the boundaries of the sea, and owned the cattle on a thousand hills was born into a family that couldn't afford a lamb . . . [who] probably struggled to put food on the table consistently."[1]

Oh that Jesus would be born into the human story at all! And to this poor, lowly family? Poet John Milton writes:

> That glorious form, that light insufferable,
> And that far-beaming blaze of majesty,
> Wherewith he wont at Heaven's high
> council-table
> To sit the midst of Trinal Unity,
> He laid aside, and, here with us to be
> Forsook the courts of everlasting day,
> And chose with us this darksome house of
> mortal clay.[2]

The Son of God, accustomed to sitting at heaven's "high table" alongside Father and Spirit, has come as the son of ordinary humans in Mary and Joseph. The Word of God is no longer thundering from the heavens or using go-betweens like priests or prophets; he is an infant crying for his mom. The one who holds the universe together with a word is born as a helpless baby needing to be fed, clothed, changed—a human who will need sleep and food to survive, who will need to learn how to walk and speak, who will fall down and cut his knee. The majestic King of heaven will grow up as the son of lower-class parents in the small, remote village of Nazareth. The Ancient of Days crosses a threshold into the limits of human history—willing to take on all the weakness of our humanity, "this darksome house of mortal clay."

The ordinary, messy, and human quality of Jesus's birth is good news for those of us who lead ordinary, messy, human lives. It tells us that our God is not a theological concept, an ancient artifact, or an academic idea. He is a *person*. He is not a cosmic deity perched in a lofty, faraway temple but a God who lovingly writes himself into our story. He understands. He gets it.

The birth narrative also shows us that God is not only after our shiny, Sunday-morning selves; he wants our commonplace, chaotic in-between too. The God of the Bible is not a god who can't be bothered with your everyday human struggles but one who came to share in them in order to bring you to himself (Heb. 4:15–16). You can bring him anything and everything. You can bring him your *real* life.

Even today, even in this very moment, he is bending low to meet you.

RESPOND IN PRAYER

Jesus, forgive me for embracing your "cosmic-ness" at the exclusion of your humanity. Forgive me for making you into a concept I can keep at arm's length, rather than a relational person who comes close. Thank you for forsaking "the courts of everlasting day" to enter my real, human story. Today I approach your throne of grace with boldness, remembering the humanity of my High Priest. Amen.

(Spend time now being "real" with God. Use real words. Talk like you really talk. Don't keep him at a distance.)

Ragged shepherds were watching their sheep that night
When the angel chorus, filled the sky with light
"Good news, great joy to this broken land
For the baby in the manger is Christ the Lamb!"

See the wise men journey from countries far
Over deserts and mountains following that star
They gave him their gifts, and bowed on their knees
For the baby in the manger is Christ the King!

Hallelujah, Christ is born!
Hallelujah, the Savior of the world
This is the One we've waited for!
Hallelujah, Hallelujah, Christ is born!

Come and bow in wonder and prepare him room
Come and sing with joy over God's good news
Go tell it on the mountain and in countries far
That the baby in the manger is the King of our hearts

from "Hallelujah, Christ Is Born"
by Caroline Cobb

Good News for All People

Read Luke 2:8–20; Matthew 2:1–18

On the world stage, it was hardly newsworthy: a back-alley birth, a poor Jewish baby, an unknown pair of teenagers far from home. But in the halls of heaven? A roar of joy was rising, erupting, spilling over: *"At last! At last!"*

In the quiet of the night, heaven's exuberance breaks into time and space. An angel chorus appears to a ragged group of shepherds, filling the sky with light as they praised God: "Glory to God in the highest heaven, and peace on earth to people he favors!" (Luke 2:14).

But why did these heralds of heaven appear to *shepherds*? Why not share the news of this royal birth with King Herod or with the religious elite like the scribes and chief priests? After all, shepherds were lower-class and uneducated, and some commentators even believe they were considered ceremoniously unclean because of their work.[3] In other words, they possessed no religious, social, or economic status. In fact, these shepherds were some of the lowest of the low in all three categories. Why were they the first to hear this good news of great joy?

Meanwhile, a group of wise men from the Far East traverse miles and miles over deserts and mountains, following a star they believe will lead them to the king of the Jews. Imagine them arriving in Jerusalem after their long journey: walking through the city in their exotic garb, their camels laden with gold and other treasures fit for royalty. These people would not have looked or sounded like Jews. They were Gentiles from pagan—or even enemy—lands. The Jews probably viewed them with a mixture of disdain and curiosity. Their first stop is, naturally, King Herod's palace. But then, the star they had followed out of the East leads them away from the courts of power, away from the big city, away from the important influencers. And when at last they find Jesus, this humblest of kings, they fall on their knees and worship with joy, gladly giving Jesus their costliest treasures.

Again, we must ask *why*. Why would God reveal the Christ to these pagan foreigners from the East? Why does he choose to write such strange characters—shepherds and Gentiles—into this story? Why do these outcasts and outsiders figure so prominently in Jesus's birth narrative? After the long silence of exile, why did God choose to speak in this way?

Theologian Andreas Köstenberger answers this way: "Just as the worship of the *magoi* pointed forward to Jesus's ethnically universal rule (encompassing both Jew and Gentile), the message to the shepherds points forward to an accessibility that depends not upon one's status (religious or socioeconomic), position, wealth, or prestige."[4]

In other words, this good news of great joy is for all people. The beauty of the gospel of Jesus is that we do not—indeed, we *cannot*—earn God's favor by appealing to our reputation, ancestry, religious activity, or tribe. It is a gift we receive only by sheer grace, through faith.

In the Christmas story, the wise men and shepherds receive the good news about Jesus and respond in faith. But sadly, others simply *miss it*. The religious leaders, for example, take the time to answer Herod's questions about Messianic

Scripture, but then it seems they keep going about their business, uninterested in looking into the birth for themselves (Matt. 3:4–6). King Herod also fails to grasp the good news by clinging even tighter to his power and godlike status, bent on destroying every potential rival (Matt. 2:16–18). The lowly shepherds and foreign wise men, on the other hand, are not distracted by power, status, or busy religious activity. Stripped of these things, they seem to have a greater capacity to receive the gospel. We see them dropping everything, hurrying to see what God has done, falling down in worship, and then—in the case of the shepherds—proceeding to share about this newborn king with everyone they meet!

So, who are we in this story then? Are we like Herod—afraid of losing our status or our carefully curated kingdoms? Or are we more like the religious leaders—too busy working for God, too self-righteous to need a Savior?

Are you like the shepherds and wise men, open and ready to receive and respond to the good news of Christ's coming? Or will you miss it?

This Advent, do not miss the good news. Do not be too busy, too self-righteous, too self-sufficient. Do not be so smitten with your social standing, economic status, or religious reputation that you miss the gospel of Jesus.

Today, hear the angel's pronouncement again, but imagine he is speaking directly to *you*:

> "I bring *you* good news that will cause great
> joy . . . Today in the town of David a Savior
> has been born to *you*; he is the Messiah, the
> Lord." (Luke 2:10–11 NIV, emphasis added)

How do you receive these words? Ask God to help you savor this good news of great joy as Christmas draws nearer. Confess your tendency to be like Herod or the religious leaders. And ask him to help you practice these behaviors instead: the exuberant worship of the angels, the costly allegiance of the wise men, the uninhibited evangelism of the shepherds.

RESPOND IN PRAYER

God, thank you for your good news
of great joy for all people! Whatever I
would boast in—status, self-sufficiency,
religious activity, tribe—I lay down. I
count everything as loss compared to the
surpassing worth of knowing you (Phil.
3:8). As I lay these down, fill me instead
with the exuberant worship of the angels,
the costly allegiance of the wise men,
and the uninhibited evangelism of the
shepherds. Amen.

Lo, he has come
To rebuild the ruins!
Lo, he has come
To set them captives free!

I know he has come
To bind up the broken
It's the year of his favor
The year of Jubilee!

from "Pave Every Road"
by Caroline Cobb

The New and Better Jubilee

Read Isaiah 61:1–3; Luke 4:16–21

Picture Jesus. He is now thirty years old, known in his small village only as a simple carpenter, the good-hearted and hardworking son of Joseph and Mary. Jesus has been quiet about his mission, but today he will speak. Today everything will change.

The community is gathered for synagogue when Jesus stands to read the Scriptures. See him slowly unrolling the scroll of Isaiah, running his finger across the parchment, searching for the words he will read. Then he begins:

> The Spirit of the Lord is on me, because
> he has anointed me to preach good news

to the poor. He has sent me to proclaim
release to the captives and recovery of sight
to the blind, to set free the oppressed, to
proclaim the year of the Lord's favor. (Luke
4:18–19)[5]

A hush fell over the crowd as Jesus sits down, the customary posture of a teacher. In the synagogue, a reading from Scripture was typically followed by an explanation of the text.[6] So the people waited. Every eye is fixed on him; everyone in the room is wondering what Joseph's son might say next.

Then Jesus declared, "Today as you listen, this Scripture has been fulfilled" (Luke 4:21).

Audible gasps come from the crowd. Jesus's statement would have been *shocking*. Here, Joseph's blue-collar carpenter son is making an earth-shattering claim: *"I am the anointed Messiah of which Isaiah spoke, sent to fulfill the mission of God."* He was the promised seed of Eve, the Righteous Branch, the Son of David, the Light of the world they had ached for in all their years of exile and foreign occupation. Nothing would be the same for Jesus again.

And what is equally astonishing? *What Jesus stops short of saying.*

Isaiah 61:2 says the Messiah would "proclaim the year of the LORD's favor, *and* the day of our God's vengeance" (emphasis added). But Jesus makes a full stop after the words "the year of the LORD's favor," leaving off the latter phrase. What could this mean?

Prophets like Isaiah assumed these two realities—favor and judgment—would happen all at once. But God has written a surprisingly different storyline in Jesus, graciously stretching the sequence of events across the wide span between his first advent and his second.[7]

The first advent of Jesus inaugurates a long period of God's favor and grace. The Hebrew "year of Jubilee" is in view here: every forty-nine years, slaves were to be set free, property returned, land and farmers given rest from sowing and reaping (Lev. 25). God designed the Jubilee as a time set aside for grace and rest, deliverance and freedom, restoration and rejoicing! Imagine being a servant working out in your master's field, so far away from family and home, and hearing the news: *"It's the Jubilee! Your debt is paid! You are free to rest and feast!"* In synagogue that day, Jesus is proclaiming and ushering in *a new and better Jubilee.*

The second coming of Jesus, on the other hand, will bring about the latter phrase of Isaiah 61. According to the Bible, the terrifying "day of vengeance" will happen. Christ *will* appear again to "judge the living and the dead" (2 Tim. 4:1), and each of us will stand before his judgment seat to "give an account of himself to God" (Rom. 14:12). Understandably, this idea makes us uncomfortable, but Jesus himself warns us:

> When the Son of Man comes in his glory, and all the angels with him, then he will sit on his glorious throne. All the nations will be gathered before him, and he will separate them one from another, just as a shepherd separates the sheep from the goats. (Matt. 25:31–32)

But notice the difference in the time spans! Do you see it? While God's reckoning and judgment will occur in something like a *day*, the time of his favor is likened to a *year*. Compared to a year, a day is almost nothing. This difference speaks to God's character: he is just and righteous, but he is also slow to anger, abounding in love, patient with the sinner, ready with forgiveness. Right now, we are living in a long "year" of God's favor. Jesus's arrival has kicked off a prolonged season of Jubilee! A day of righteous judgment is inevitably coming . . . but not yet.

Even now, Jesus offers freedom from our slavery to sin (Rom. 6:15–23), forgiveness of debts (Col. 2:14), and rest for the work-weary soul (Matt. 11:28–30). Even now, he is welcoming us into the abundance and joy of God's presence.

Through his birth, life, death, and resurrection, Jesus has flung wide the door of God's mercy—an open invitation for all who would accept: "Come into my Father's joy and favor, both now and into eternity!"

In Advent, we acknowledge that we live in the liminal space between "the year of his favor" in Isaiah 61:2a and "the day of vengeance" in Isaiah 61:2b. We rejoice that Jesus has ushered in a long year of Jubilee with his birth, even as we recognize a day of reckoning is just over the horizon. We must hold both truths in tension and let both realities transform how we live. Ask yourself: Are you living in light of both? Do you live as if you *actually* expect Jesus to come back? Do you live as if the gospel, this undeserved welcome into God's favor, is *really* true?

As Christians, we should take great joy at Jesus's invitation into God's eternal grace and favor—the Jubilee made possible by Jesus Christ! But the reality of his day of justice means we dare not take it for granted. It also means we dare not keep it to ourselves. Advent invites us to recognize just how good the proclamation of Jesus really is and just how inevitable his return, and then to live in such a way that takes both realities into account.

RESPOND IN PRAYER

God, let me be reverent in my joy, sober-minded in my hope, and urgent in my mission to invite others into the joy of your presence, the long year of your favor. Let me not take this grace, this access, for granted: to be welcomed into the place where the Holy God dwells. Thank you for Jesus, the new and better Jubilee. Let me be a herald of this good news even today, with (list one or two names). Amen.

The Spirit of the Lord is on you
A King anointed for the cross
To the helpless you bring good news
You come to bind the broken heart

Speaking freedom to the captives
Comfort to the ones who grieve
To the downcast you bring justice
To the needy ones relief

from "The Year of His Favor"
by Caroline Cobb

DAY 18

A King Anointed for a Mission

Read Isaiah 61:1–3; Luke 4:16–30

That fateful day in Nazareth, Jesus boldly claims to be the promised Messiah the people had ached for in all their long years of exile, a King anointed by the Spirit of God for a specific mission. But what will his mission be? And why do we need it? Jesus reminds us that our need is much deeper than we realize, but his mission is also better and more expansive than we could ever imagine.

To bring good news to the poor . . .

The Messiah's promise in Isaiah 61 would have sounded like good news to the impoverished exiles; they had likely lost everything when foreign armies invaded. And when Jesus spoke these words to his community in Nazareth many years later, his listeners may have thought of how Rome's oppressive taxes were bleeding them dry and how the Messiah would grant them financial relief. But with Jesus, this promise of good news expands beyond material poverty to something deeper: a poverty of spirit (Matt. 5:3).

Nancy Guthrie writes, "Jesus wanted them to see that to be poor in spirit—to be keenly aware that they are powerless and bankrupt and have nothing to offer to God to get in his good graces—is what would prepare them to receive God's riches."[8]

In Jesus's upside-down economy where need is all you need, "only the beggar will have the currency."[9] Only those who acknowledge their impoverished state as sinners and their desperate need for grace will see the gospel of Jesus for what it is: good news. Today, are you aware of your poverty of spirit? Are you able to see just how good this news about Jesus really is?

To bind up the brokenhearted . . .

These word "to bind"or "heal" also appear in Isaiah 1, when the prophet describes the desolation of God's people: "From the sole of the foot even to the head, no spot is unin-jured—wounds, welts, and festering sores not cleansed, ban-daged, or soothed with oil" (Isa. 1:6).

The prophets tell us the wounds of the exiles were self-inflicted, a result of their faithless turning away from God. And yet, God will not leave them alone to suffer, however much they deserve it. His compassionate heart compels him to bind up their brokenness, even at great cost to himself.

Here we see the Messiah comes not to the flawless and healthy but to the wounded and limping, the ones with their hearts in pieces. Picture him as a kind physician, gently applying balm to your brokenness. By his wounds, even our deepest wounds are healed (Isa. 53:5). Today, are you willing to admit your brokenhearted longing, your need for his bandaging and binding?

To proclaim liberty to the captives and the oppressed . . .

Writing to future exiles, Isaiah comforts with promises of deliverance from a physical captivity, justice for those oppressed by pagan rulers, and a return home to Jerusalem. But with Jesus, these comforting promises signify a much deeper reality: we were captive to sin and the tyranny of Satan, but Jesus "rescued us from the domain of darkness and transferred us into the kingdom of the Son he loves" (Col. 1:13). On the earth, Jesus would free the captives in a physical and even a social sense as well: healing the sick, casting out demons, touching the unclean, drawing near to the outcast. He is proclaiming freedom for both body and soul, physical and spiritual. Today, will you own up to the heavy shackles holding you captive? Your deep need for a freedom only Jesus can bring?

To proclaim the year of God's favor to the nations . . .

While this aspect of the Messiah's mission is not explicit in Isaiah 61:1–3, Jesus makes it central in Luke 4. After Jesus says, "Today as you listen, this Scripture has been fulfilled," his hometown community reacts by marveling at his words. But they seem more flabbergasted than angry. That is, until he picks up the topic of the Gentiles.

In Luke 4:24, Jesus begins talking about Elijah and Elisha, pointing to the way they ministered to Gentiles like the widow in Zarephath (1 Kings 17:8–24) and Naaman (a Syrian ruler and leper; 2 Kings 5:1–14). And suddenly, his community's marveling becomes nothing less than seething rage. They forcibly drive Jesus out of town, intending to throw him off the edge of a cliff to his death. They are infuriated by the idea that their Messiah would come for the whole world. But Jesus was Isaiah's "banner to the peoples," a rallying point for the people of God from every tribe and tongue, the hope of both Jews and Gentiles (Isa. 11:10; 49:22; 62:10). Do you realize what a grace it is that God has welcomed you to himself through Jesus? Or have you grown ho-hum about "For God so loved the world" (John 3:16 KJV)?

A King anointed for the cross . . .

Ultimately, King Jesus was anointed for the cross, leading to his resurrection and ours. As we receive the good news of Luke 4 and Isaiah 61 as a gift, the most fitting response is to turn and share this good news with others—in our local community and across the globe.

During Advent, we make ready for our King to come. We make ready by first *acknowledging our great need*—our poverty, brokenness, captivity—in order to prime ourselves for his healing and freedom. Our needs are deep, but his grace always runs deeper (Rom. 5:20). We also make ready by *practicing our calling as heralds of his kingdom*. In every season, we raise high the banner of Jesus's gospel, calling the whole world to rally to his gracious rule, to come and receive beauty for ashes. And in his power, we speak good news to the poor, bind up the brokenhearted, and proclaim freedom to the captives and grace to every nation.

> How beautiful on the mountains are the feet of the herald, who proclaims peace, who brings news of good things, who proclaims salvation, who says to Zion, "Your God reigns!" (Isa. 52:7)

RESPOND IN PRAYER

God, I was bankrupt in sin, but you sent
Jesus to pay my debt. I was blind, but
you opened my eyes to behold you. I was
enslaved to Satan's tyrannical rule, but
through Christ you have flung the prison
doors open and set me free. God, help
me rejoice in the good news and treasure
you as my Redeemer. Let this joy compel
me to share your gospel with the world,
to proclaim the year of your favor and
grace. Amen.

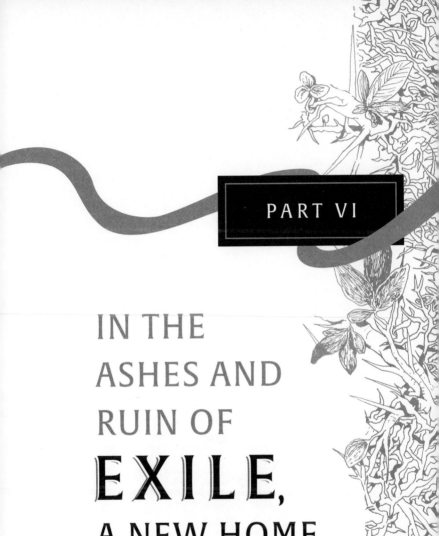

PART VI

IN THE
ASHES AND
RUIN OF
EXILE,
A NEW HOME
FOR GOD

You give beauty for ashes
You pour out the oil of gladness
The year of his favor comes
The year of his favor!

You give to the weak and faint
A garment of joy and praise
The year of his favor comes!

Come, Lord! Come, Lord!

from "The Year of His Favor"
by Caroline Cobb

Beauty for the Ashes of Mourning

Read James 4:8–10; Luke 15:11–24

> "The Spirit of the Lord GOD is on me . . .
> to comfort all who mourn." (Isa. 61:1–2)

Yet another aspect of Jesus's mission as Messiah would be to comfort all who mourn. But who exactly are these mourners in Isaiah 61, and why are they so sad?

C. H. Spurgeon points out that these grieving people are "in Zion" and looking to God for comfort. In other words, it is not the unfaithful sinners who are mourning but the faithful remnant back in Zion after exile.[1] These people have so much to be sad about: the ruin of their city, the death of their loved ones, the loss of their former life. But none of these is the primary cause of their mourning in this passage. They are grieving over *sin*. In his commentary on Isaiah 61, J. Alec Motyer writes, "Mourning over sin [is] the primary thought and means of entering into the following blessings."[2] Here, the blessing of God's comfort is reserved for the contrite, the ones willing to call sin what it is and weep.

Like the faithful in Zion, God's people today should *mourn*. Over our own idolatry and rebellion against God. Over the sin we see in the world around us. Over the brokenness and ugly divisions within Jesus's church. Over all the ways his kingdom is yet to come "on earth as it is in heaven" (Matt. 6:10). Do you grieve this way?

Remember, this type of mourning is *good*. Spurgeon describes it as a mark of grace and a means of Christ's comfort: "To mourn after more holiness is a sign of holiness, to mourn after greater conformity to the image of Christ proves that we are already in a measure conformed thereunto; to sigh after more complete subordination of our entire life to the will of God is a mourning for which Jesus Christ will bring rich comfort."[3]

Do you see the beautiful promise here? This type of mourning will be met with the comfort of Jesus himself!

This is what Jesus meant when he said, "blessed are those who mourn, for they shall be comforted" (Matt. 5:4). Yes, it's true that as pilgrims and exiles on the earth Christians might experience an "enlarged heritage of mourning."[4] But this righteous mourning gives us the capacity for a better, truer comfort. This type of grief carves out a canyon through which the river of God's grace can flow.

In modern Western culture, mourners at funerals typically dress in dark blacks and greys—an outward signal of their inner sorrow. In the ancient Near East, a person in mourning would use even more involved visuals to signal their sorrow: intentionally wearing an uncomfortable sackcloth, sitting in dust and ashes, tearing their robes, fasting from food, and refusing to wash or anoint themselves with oil. Again, they are allowing their outward appearance to mirror their interior state and even viscerally move them into more grief.

King David mourned in this way, fasting and refusing to get up from the ground, when he knew his son by Bathsheba would die as a result of his sinful choice (2 Sam. 12:13–23). The king of Nineveh also mourned in this way—removing his robe, sitting in ashes, calling for a nationwide fast—when Jonah called him to repentance (Jonah 3:4–10).

During the desolation of exile, God uses the outward state of Jerusalem and Judah's countryside to make visible the inward, spiritual reality of his people. The land was scorched, dry and over-run with thorns. The temple was ripped to pieces and burned with fire. The whole of Judah, as it were, was forced to sit in dust and ashes. In turn, the faithful remnant in Zion acknowledged their sin and need. In his justice, God had every right to end their story here, to leave them lying in the bed they had made. *But he doesn't!* Instead, he promises to comfort them in their mourning, giving them beauty for their ashes.

They did not yet realize the shape this comfort would take, but we know it now: Jesus is the comfort of God in human form. Grieving sinners, unsure of how God might respond to their brokenness, need only look to Jesus. Hear the good news:

In Jesus, God meets our proper grief over sin with undeserved, abundant *joy*. When we sprinkle dust and ashes on our heads, God grants us a crown of beauty (Isa. 61:3). When we admit all our righteousness is like filthy rags, God clothes us with Christ's robe of righteousness and a garment of praise (Isa. 64:6; 61:10). When we say we have no right to get up from our place of mourning, God lifts us out of the shadows and lavishly anoints us with the oil of gladness (Isa. 61:3). And this is no small drip of joy either! His oil of gladness is *pouring out* in abundance. This is extravagant, abundant, limitless, unbridled! Grace upon grace upon grace.

———

Picture yourself as the prodigal son returning home: dressed in rags, head hung low, knowing you are unworthy, rehearsing your apology: "Father, I have sinned against heaven and in your sight" (Luke 15:18, 21). Do you hear the pounding of your father's footsteps as he runs to meet you? Can you feel his arms around your skin-and-bones frame before you can even get out a word? His kiss on your sunken cheek? Soon, his servants are dressing you: wrapping you in his best robe, putting shoes on your feet and the family ring on your finger. Someone helps you wash your face and anoints you with oil. You catch a glimpse of yourself in the mirror, and the tears come fast. Do you see it? *You are dressed like a son again.*

When righteous grief strips us bare, we see more clearly the goodness of the gospel and the comfort we have through Christ.

One day, mourning will be no more. God himself will wipe away every tear. And clothed in white, the bride of Christ will take up the song of Isaiah's Messiah:

I rejoice greatly in the L ORD, I exult in my God; for he has clothed me with the garments of salvation and wrapped me in a robe of righteousness. (Isa. 61:10)

RESPOND IN PRACTICE

What would it look like for you to have righteous grief over your sin? Advent is an invitation to mourn in order to receive the comfort of Christ. Do a quick Internet search for Rembrandt's famous painting, *Return of the Prodigal Son*. As you look at this painting, try to imagine yourself in the son's place—ragged and dirty, desperate and kneeling—but also embraced, forgiven, restored, and so very loved! How would you feel receiving your Father's robe, his kiss, his arms around you? Respond to this imaginative exercise through prayer.[5]

You come to raise up what's been ruined
Rivers in a desert waste
You are the Lord and you will do this
For the glory of your name!

from "The Year of His Favor"
by Caroline Cobb

Let us go with our Lord to the margins
To the broken, the poor and the lost
By his Spirit, we'll push back the darkness
Let his church take up her cross

Come help us, Lord Jesus to love as you loved
As we remember your gospel, how you first loved us
To seek justice, love mercy and care for the weak
To live now in light of the kingdom we seek

from "Let It Be So With Your Church"
by Caroline Cobb

Who Will Rebuild the Ruins?

Read Isaiah 61:1–11

> "They will rebuild the ancient ruins; they
> will restore the former devastations; they
> will renew the ruined cities, the devasta-
> tions of many generations." (Isa. 61:4)

Yesterday, we explored how God gives comfort to the ones who mourn. Today, we see that he gives them more than just comfort; he gives them a *mission*.

Notice that in Isaiah 61:1–3, the servant of the Lord is speaking, talking about what *he* will do. Sent by God and anointed by the Spirit, the Messiah will proclaim, heal, comfort, provide. But in verse 4, the subject of the sentence suddenly shifts. The action verbs stem from someone new. Who will rebuild the ancient ruins? Who will restore and renew the generational devastation? "*They* will."

Pastor Ray Ortlund points out that the antecedent to "they" in verse 4 comes from verse 3: "the ones who mourn in Zion."[6] God intends to bring restoration and renewal, but this is not a solo project for the Messiah. Neither will it be accomplished by the typical front-runners: the strong, the self-sufficient, the powerful and elite. In an unexpected plot twist, God says he will use the *mourners* to rebuild the ruins. Verse 1 reminds us that "they" are also the poor and needy, the brokenhearted, the captives sitting in darkness.

This promise finds partial fulfillment in the books of Ezra and Nehemiah, when the exiles were slowly returning to Jerusalem. When Ezra realized the depths of the sin of God's people, he tore his tunic and his robe, then fell face down in front of the house of God, weeping and offering a humble prayer of confession. The people follow suit, weeping bitterly over their sin (Ezra 9:3–10:16). Nehemiah 9 records a large gathering that ends in national confession—fasting in sackcloth, dust on their heads. Ezra and Nehemiah's leadership, coupled with the reading of God's Word, compel the people of God to confess their sins and renew their covenant vows.

Here, we see a people fully aware of their weakness and sin, a people who realize there's no point in pretense or hiding. They've given up on trying to prove their own worth or goodness. Here, we see a people with no choice left but to cast themselves upon the mercy of God. And when they do, God not only meets them with forgiveness, but he also entrusts them with a work. These same mourners would literally rebuild God's city after the devastation of exile. Stone by stone. Brick by brick.

But the promises of Isaiah 61 extend far beyond the physical rebuilding of Jerusalem we see under Ezra and Nehemiah. God is building a spiritual kingdom—one that will one day culminate in a new creation, a final home for his presence. And over and over in the Bible, we find God doing this kingdom-building work in and through the ones who boast in grace alone. The Messiah's mission of restoration will be carried out by a people who confess their need, then throw themselves headlong onto the gospel of Jesus, determined to live and work in humble dependence on his Spirit.

C. S. Lewis describes a "vital moment" in which we "turn to God and say, 'You must do this. I can't.'" He continues, "It is the change from being confident about our own efforts to the state in which we despair of doing anything for ourselves and leave it to God."[7]

God's mourners experience this "vital moment." The desolate vineyard growing only bitter grapes cries, *"You must do this; we can't!"* God answers by grafting them into a Righteous Branch and saying, "They will be called oaks of righteousness, a planting of the LORD for the display of his splendor" (Isa. 61:3 NIV). The people who had failed their mission as *imago Dei* to the world confess, *"You must do this; we can't!"* And God answers, "You will be called the LORD's priests. . . . And as a garden enables what is sown to spring up, so the Lord GOD will cause righteousness and praise to spring up before all the nations" (Isa. 61:6, 11).

See Jacob walking with a limp and Moses with his tongue tied. Picture Peter, the rock on which Jesus will build his church, sinking beneath the waves and denying Christ three times. Look at Paul with his murderous past and that troublesome thorn in his side. All reached Lewis's "vital moment." All were "mourners" in one way or another, fully aware of their insufficiencies and failure. And yet, in some mysterious way, this awareness made them more useful to God's kingdom mission, not less. As Jesus reminds Paul, "My grace is sufficient for you, for my power is perfected in weakness" (2 Cor. 12:9).

Hear this today: God does not send the squeaky-clean who seem (or pretend) to have it all together. He is not a coach trying to "stack the team," recruiting only the brightest and best to build his kingdom. In fact, the opposite is true. He is after the ones who look to him and say, *"You must do this! I can't!"* God delights to work through this type of person. In fact, if the gospel is true, this is the *only* way he works through us at all.

God is inviting you into his mission, even—no, *especially*—in your weakness, when you reach that "vital moment" and acknowledge you have nothing to boast in but him. So, go! Speak the good news and walk in the good works God has put in front of you to do (Eph. 2:10). Then, watch in wonder as he brings the fruitfulness of Eden to the barrenness of exile all around you, causing righteousness and praise to spring up like bright flowers in a garden. Watch and see how God ministers and moves—both in and through you—to rebuild, restore, renew. Stone by stone and brick by brick.

RESPOND IN PRACTICE

Isaiah's call in Isaiah 6:1–8 is a good model for us as we consider what it takes to be "fit" for the mission of God. Hear Isaiah cry, "Woe is me!" and "Here I am. Send me." How did he get from one phrase to the other? As God atones for our sin through Christ, God atoned for Isaiah's sin through a burning coal taken from the altar. God made him "fit" for the task at hand. As hymnist Joseph Hart wrote, "All the fitness he requires is to feel your need of him."[8]

Use Isaiah's response to God's call as a prompt for your own response. Let your "woe is me" propel you to savor the goodness of the gospel. And let the goodness of the gospel propel you to say, "Here I am! Send me!"

Lift up your head! Be on the lookout!
Wake from your bed! Don't fall asleep!
Lift up your head! He's comin' soon now!
Get yourself ready for the comin' of the King!

Could a mother forget her children?
Could a husband forget his wife?
How much more then, will he remember?
Will he come and set things right!

Cast aside all the works of darkness
Live as children of the day
Light your lamps and keep them burnin'
Till we see our bridegroom's face

---

from "Be on the Lookout!"
by Caroline Cobb

Light Your Lamps!

Read: Matthew 25:1–13

> "It is already the hour for you to wake up
> from sleep, because now our salvation is
> nearer than when we first believed. The
> night is nearly over, and the day is near;
> so let us discard the deeds of darkness
> and put on the armor of light."
> (Rom. 13:11–12)

Advent is a season set aside for waiting and watching for the Messiah. But what does this waiting actually look like, day-to-day? As the people of God, how are we to stay awake and ready? We wait well through the long night by keeping our lamps burning and by living as people of the light, not the darkness.

WAKE UP! KEEP YOUR LAMPS BURNING!

In Jesus's time, the marriage custom called for the groom to travel to the bride's home for the wedding, often at night. Afterward, the wedding party would take up their lamps and escort the couple back to the groom's home for a celebratory feast.[9] In our reading from Matthew 25 today, Jesus tells of ten bridesmaids waiting for a groom to arrive. But he seems to be running late! The bridesmaids are drowsy, growing less alert by the hour. Eventually they're all asleep. When the groom comes at last, waking them from their slumber, five realize they did not bring enough oil for their lamps and are forced to make a quick trip to the store. Jesus tells us the five unprepared bridesmaids end up missing the party entirely.

This story is a warning and a wake-up call. If we really believe Jesus the Bridegroom is returning, we must remain awake and ready. Elsewhere, Jesus says, "Stay dressed for action and keep your lamps burning" (Luke 12:35 ESV).

In her book *Advent*, Fleming Rutledge poses two important questions with regard to this parable: What fuel is currently in our lamps? And what kind of oil do we need to keep them burning? She writes, "Telling the [Bible's] story in a nostalgic way as though it were a nice fairy tale for the children won't work anymore. . . . If we try to do that, we will wake up at midnight and discover that *our lamps are going out*. Sentiment, nostalgia, optimism: these are weak, thin fuels. We need premium oil for our lamps if we are to keep the light of the church burning in the time of trial. Christianity is not for sissies."[10]

In these dark days of exile, we need real fuel. We pray and read God's Word—not to dig up a few therapeutic nuggets for our day but to ignite a sustained faith. We go to church—not to check the box or because it makes us feel good but because it's where we resupply the oil we need to keep our lamps burning. Here we rehearse the gospel story week after week: we let the Word preached confront and convict and console us, we sing together of our strong hope, we participate in the sacraments. Between Sundays, we prod one another out of lethargic, sentimental religion and onward to love and good deeds (Heb. 10:24). We all get sleepy and tired of waiting sometimes, but this is why we must be part of a community of other Christians. Today might be a day for poking your drowsy friend in the ribs or asking them to do the same for you. Community itself is fuel.

But in this conversation about oil, we are still missing a central character: the Holy Spirit. As we saw with the story of King David on day 11, oil in Scripture often symbolizes the indwelling of the Spirit to consecrate and empower someone for a God-given task. If you are in Christ, you have the penultimate power source readily available to you, God's very presence dwelling within you (John 14:16–17; Rom. 8:9)! As you tend your lamp to keep it burning, the Holy Spirit works to warm you to God's ways and to set your heart ablaze for his glory.

WAKE UP! LIVE LIKE CHILDREN OF THE DAY!

The story of the ten sleepy bridesmaids takes place in the dead of night. So too, prophets like Isaiah compare the exile to a long darkness, the faithful aching for the Messiah like a sunrise. The apostle Paul, writing to God's new people, also picks up this light-versus-dark motif to underscore their new identity and way of being.[11]

We once belonged to the domain of darkness, but through Jesus, God has brought us into his kingdom of light (Col. 1:13). We once belonged to the night, but now we are children of the day (1 Thess. 5:5). Paul calls us to live in alignment with our new identity by actively casting away the works of darkness and putting on the light of Christ (Rom. 13:11–12).

We acknowledge this is an incredibly unnatural thing to do. After all, like the bridesmaids and the exiles, we still live out our lives in the darkness before the dawn. And isn't it so *tempting* to fall asleep, to get careless, to lose our counter-cultural shine? Again, Paul shakes us awake with an Advent reminder: "The night is nearly over, and the day is near" (Rom. 13:12) The sun is already rising just over the horizon; Jesus the Bridegroom is coming soon!

The call to live like "children of the day" in this "domain of darkness" is a call into the uncomfortable life of an exile. If you are following Christ, people will think you are strange, and, in turn, you will often feel like a stranger.

Poet T. S. Eliot illustrates this point in "Journey of the Magi." In it, he imagines what the wise men might have felt once they returned home after seeing the infant Jesus:

> This: were we led all that way for
> Birth or Death? There was a Birth, certainly
> We had evidence and no doubt. I had seen
>   birth and death,

But had thought they were different; this
> Birth was
Hard and bitter agony for us, like Death, our
> death.
We returned to our places, these Kingdoms,
But no longer at ease here, in the old
> dispensation,
With an alien people clutching their gods.
I should be glad of another death.[12]

As Christians, we are no longer at ease here in the old kingdom. As children of light, we are no longer at ease in the darkness. We will not feel at home here until God makes his home with us in the new creation. We are a people longing for the Sun to rise and the Bridegroom to return.

So wake up! Be on the lookout! Get the right oil in your lamps and keep your lamp burning! God's Story is no fairy tale; it's *true*. And you know how it ends: the Sun will rise; the Bridegroom will come. Cast aside the works of darkness and make ready. *Wake up!*

RESPOND IN PRACTICE

Consider the spiritual disciplines as oil for your lamp, keeping you awake and oriented to Christ as you wait for his return. Are there fuel sources you might not be availing yourself of, or areas in which you might want to grow (i.e., prayer, fasting, Sabbath, Bible reading, worship, church involvement, etc.)? Are there thin, weak fuels you need to give up (i.e., mindless scrolling or consumption of media, a sinful habit or addiction you need to bring into the light, etc.)? Write out your response to these questions in a journal. Consider telling a friend about your answers and asking them to keep you accountable, "poking you in the ribs" when you are tempted to fall asleep.

See those fields, they're ripe for harvest
See the work that's left undone
Take to the world his love and justice
Singin' "let his kingdom come!"
Oh let his kingdom come!

from "Be on the Lookout!"
by Caroline Cobb

Let it be so with your church, Oh God
We are your hands and feet!
As Jesus bent low to serve in love
So with us let it be! So with us let it be!

from "Let It Be So With Your Church"
by Caroline Cobb

Planting Seeds for the New Eden

Read Titus 2:11–14; Galatians 6:7–10

Like most kids, our three hate to wait. According to them, waiting is "boring" because "there is nothing to do!" I feel like this sometimes too, especially when I am waiting to board a plane or see a doctor. I find myself scrolling on my phone, flipping through an old magazine, wasting time. Waiting can feel pointless, inefficient, and, yes, *boring*.

But Advent's call to wait and watch for Christ's return is different. It is not a passive staring off into the distance. It is not an excuse to sit back or lie low until the real action begins.

And our life as exiles should not feel like the pointless loitering of a doctor's waiting area or an airport terminal, as if the world is merely a holding room until we get called up to heaven.

Fleming Rutledge writes, "Believing that God will come does not imply inaction. Rather, it stirs up the church to hopeful enactments of the reign of Christ. Everything we do in this regard, however small, from AIDS ministry to overseas missions, strikes a blow against the usurping powers and principalities until Jesus comes again in glory."[13]

Waiting on the Lord is active because we live in the "already" of God's new creation, even as we wait for it to be fully realized. As the people of God, we eagerly engage in good works as "hopeful enactments" of Christ's kingdom, pushing back the darkness and manifesting his ways and his rule "on earth as it is in heaven" (Matt. 6:10). What Rutledge describes is anything but boring or passive. And there is *so much* good work to do!

N. T. Wright picks up this theme in *Surprised by Hope*:

> What you do in the Lord is not in vain. You are not oiling the wheels of a machine that's about to roll over a cliff. You are not restoring a great painting that's shortly going to be thrown on the fire. You are not planting a rose in a garden that's about to be dug up

for a building site. You are—strange though it may seem, almost as hard to believe as the resurrection itself—accomplishing something that will become in due course part of God's new world. Every act of love, gratitude, and kindness; every work of art or music inspired by the love of God and delight in the beauty of his creation; every minute spent teaching a severely handicapped child to read or walk; every act of care and nurture, of comfort and support, for one's fellow human beings and for that matter one's fellow nonhuman creatures; and of course every prayer, all Spirit-led teaching, every deed that spreads the gospel, builds up the church, embraces and embodies holiness rather than corruption, and makes the name of Jesus honored in the world—all of this will find its way, through the resurrecting power of God, into the new creation that God will one day make. That is the logic of the mission of God."[14]

You are God's workmanship, his *poiēma*—created with a unique personality and skill set, situated in a specific place and area of influence, given certain work to walk in—all for the good of others and the glory of God (Eph. 2:10; 1 Cor. 7:17–20; Col. 3:17; 1 Pet. 4:10–11). Said another way, God has supplied you with a handful of seeds to sow and a specific plot of land to cultivate. Even now, the chief Sower is scattering the seeds of the new Eden all over the world and graciously inviting each of us to join him as joyful co-laborers (1 Cor. 3:9). Because God has given his Word and promised a harvest, we know this kind of work is not done in vain. "For just as rain and snow fall from heaven and do not return there without saturating the earth and making it germinate and sprout, and providing seed to sow and food to eat, so my word that comes from my mouth will not return to me empty, but it will accomplish what I please and will prosper in what I send it to do" (Isa. 55:10–11). "Open your eyes," Jesus says. "Look at the fields, because they are ready for harvest" (John 4:35).

Do not spend too much time overthinking your specific calling. Why not begin by looking to the patch of ground right in front of you? Then put your hand to the plow. You are filled with the Spirit, and you already have everything you need for life and godliness through Christ (2 Pet. 1:3). So just *start*. The invitation here is not the pressure-filled, pep-rally call for you to "do big things for God" in short bursts of fevered, "camp high" spirituality. Rather, this is an invitation to a farmer's "long obedience in the same direction."[15] It is a slow, patient, and often unseen work. You do not have to do it all at once.

And you do not have to do it alone! The work of *imago Dei* and going about God's mission in the world is not a project accomplished in isolation. You are a part of the church of God: "a chosen race, a royal priesthood, a holy nation, a people for his possession" (1 Pet. 2:9). You are part of the body of Christ, each part with a role to play, ever growing into his fullness (1 Cor. 12:12–26; Eph. 4:12–13). As we saw on day 1, you are a living stone fitted together with other believers to build the house of God, the place the Presence now dwells through the Spirit! (Eph. 2:21–22) Through the church, God means to finish what he started in Eden, until the whole earth is filled to bursting with his glory.

So, while you wait, roll up your sleeves and pick up a shovel. Cultivate the little plot of land right before you—your family, neighborhood, workplace. Do the small things in front of you to do. Be eager to do good works. Tell the story. Serve. Sing the song. Work hard and with all your heart (Col. 3:23). Sit with the suffering. Get your hands dirty. Seek the *shalom* of your city, the place of your exile (Jer. 7:4–7). Always sow the seed of good news, wherever you go. And pray to the Lord of the harvest. He is coming soon!

RESPOND IN PRACTICE

Grab a journal and a pen and spend some time thinking and writing on the good work God has placed in front of you. What little plot of land has God put in front of you to cultivate and tend? Into what people and circumstances around you could you sow the hope and light of Christ? Where is God already at work in your community? How can you join your local church to plant the seeds of the new Eden?

An equally important question: Is there anything you feel God is *not* calling you to do, but you keep trying to do it anyway? Write a prayer in response.

PART VII

IN OUR
PRESENT
EXILE,
A FUTURE
HOPE

There will be a day when the house of God
Like a mountain o'er the hills will be lifted up
As a river flows ever to the sea
All the nations will flow to him like a living stream

There will be a day when the Prince of Peace
Will break the bow and sword and make all wars cease
And our guns and bombs will be melted down
Into plowshares for the harvest, how we're longing for it now

There will be a day, and it's drawing near
When he'll lift the veil of death and he'll dry our tears
And with joy we'll go to his wedding feast
And his glory will fill up the earth like the waters fill the sea

When we'll go to the mountain of God
We'll walk in his ways, we'll look on his face
We'll go to the mountain of God
We'll cast down our pride and walk in his light
On the mountain of God

from "There Will Be A Day (Isaiah 2)"
by Caroline Cobb

186

We'll Go to the Mountain of God

Read Isaiah 2:1–4; Isaiah 11:6–10; Isaiah 25:6–9

In the ancient Near East, many considered mountains sacred, "the homes of the gods."[1] Zeus had Mount Olympus, the Canaanite deities had Mount Zaphon, and altars to idols were often built in "high places."[2] Even Yahweh, the one true God, met with his people at high elevation: first at Mount Sinai and then in the temple at Mount Zion. Interestingly, the prophet Ezekiel locates the garden of Eden on a mountaintop as well (Ezek. 28:13–14).[3]

The mountain motif also figures prominently in Isaiah's vision. One day, "the mountain of the house of the LORD shall be established as the highest of the mountains, and shall be lifted up above the hills" (Isa. 2:2 ESV). Here, God will make his home with his people forever. Our three passages today give us three snapshots of what this heavenly Mount Zion will be like. We will see that, because of Jesus, "the mountain of the house of the LORD" will be drastically different from Olympus or Zaphon or even the fire and storm of Sinai. It will be like Eden but better.[4]

A PLACE OF COMMUNION WITH GOD AND HIS DIVERSE PEOPLE

First, God will not be alone on Zion, high above us, thundering in his holiness as he did on Sinai. Instead, he will dwell *with* his people, bringing us into the overflowing, joyful communion of Father, Son, and Spirit—just as he did in Eden.

And God's company won't be just for Adam and Eve, nor will it be reserved for Abraham's physical descendants. Isaiah 2 paints a wider, more inclusive portrait of God's people. Like a living stream flowing uphill, people from every tribe and tongue will march up this mountain to walk in God's ways. The image of foreigners flooding into God's city would have been terribly surprising for Isaiah's original audience, as they imagined their enemies—Assyrians, Babylonians, Egyptians—welcomed in! But citizenship in God's kingdom is for *anyone* who hopes in Christ and takes refuge beneath his banner. On Mount Zion, we will worship side by side with ransomed brothers and sisters of every color, language, and people group. Together, we will find our home in God, even as he makes his home with us forever.

A PLACE OF TRUE PEACE

In chapter 11, Isaiah describes the mountain of God as a place where predatory animals like wolves and bears will dwell peacefully with the vulnerable: calves, lambs, and even little children (Isa. 11:6–9). Barry G. Webb describes this symbolic language as a picture of creation being "put back into joint," of the glory of Eden expanding to cover the whole earth.[5] For Israel—always under siege from preying nations—this beautiful image would have been very good news indeed. But Isaiah was pointing beyond earthly peace, and even beyond the first advent of Jesus to his second. Can you imagine a world without war or violence? A place where our guns and bombs are melted down into farming equipment (Isa. 2:4)? According to Motyer, the exchanging of war tools for agricultural ones is "symbolic of the return to Eden: people right with God again;

the curse removed; the end of the serpent's dominion; an ideal environment."[6] How we long for this promise to come true:

> They will not harm or destroy each other on
> my entire holy mountain, for the land will be
> as full of the knowledge of the LORD as the
> sea is filled with water. (Isa. 11:9)

AN ENEMY DESTROYED, A FEAST PREPARED

Our final passage from Isaiah 25 says,

> On this mountain, the LORD of Armies will
> prepare for all the peoples a feast of choice
> meat, a feast with aged wine, prime cuts
> of choice meat, fine vintage wine. On this
> mountain he will swallow up the burial
> shroud, the shroud over all the peoples, the
> sheet covering all the nations. When he has
> swallowed up death once and for all, the
> Lord GOD will wipe away the tears from
> every face. (Isa. 25:6–8)

Just imagine it! A weary pilgrim, you at last arrive at the heavenly Mount Zion. The table is set with the richest food and the best wine and crowded with joyful faces. The wilderness of exile—the thorny curse of sin, the homesick weeping, the darkness of death—is swallowed up at last by the garden of resurrection. God himself bends to gently wipe your tears away. *"Here! Take this seat,"* he says. *"Come and eat and drink your fill. It's free! I have paid for your place at my table"* (Isa. 55:1–3; Rev. 22:17).

Because Jesus on Gethsemane's Mount of Olives agreed to take the cup of God's holy wrath against sin, we will drink deeply of the well-aged wine of forgiveness and *shalom* on the mountain of God. Because Jesus willingly descended into death at the cross, we will one day arrive on the heights of Zion to dwell with God in everlasting life.

And on that day, we will lift our voices and raise our glasses in a toast:

> Look, this is our God;
> we have waited for him, and he has saved us.
> This is the Lord; we have waited for him.
> Let's rejoice and be glad in his salvation.
> (Isa. 25:9)

RESPOND IN PRACTICE

Remember our reflection from day 2, and
the prompt to fast from a meal in order
to pique our hunger for Christ's coming?
Tonight at dinner, do the reverse. As
you eat, take a moment to consider the
cost of the food and drink and the time
it took for you or your host to prepare
it. Pause and savor—even if it's just taco
night!—and look ahead to the day you will
sit at God's table on his mountain. As an
optional add-on, read Isaiah 55:1–2 over
the people at your table.

I see a city coming down
Like a bride in whitest gown, purely dressed
I see the pilgrims coming home
All creation finds shalom; the promised rest
The Lamb of God will be her light
The sun will have no need to shine

The Lord will banish every sin
All that's broken he will mend and make new
And we will see him face to face
As he wipes our tears away
Death is through
And all the ransomed and redeemed
From every tongue and tribe will sing

Behold! Behold! God makes his home with us!
He'll take his throne, forever glorious!
The curse will be undone
O come Lord, Jesus come!

At last the darkness will surrender to the light
But we unveiled in glory will forever shine
At last the powers of hell will drown in lakes of fire
But we will freely drink the crystal streams of life

Come thirsty taste and see
Come hungry to the feast
Come weary find your peace
The Bride and Spirit sing
"Come! Come!"

from "Behold, Behold (Revelation)"
by Caroline Cobb and Sean Aaron Carter

Behold! God Makes His Home with Us!

Read Revelation 21–22:5; Isaiah 65:17–25

During Advent, we stoke the embers of our longing, waiting and watching for God's kingdom of light to break through all the darkness. But what should the object of our longing actually be? For what are we really longing?

DEATH DEFEATED

Revelation 21–22 gives us a fuller picture of the "new heaven and new earth" that Isaiah promises. The apostle John is given a vision of a new Jerusalem, a holy city, coming down to the earth out of heaven. In this Edenic city, the Lord will banish every sin and mend every brokenness. Even the curse of death, that terrible shadow plaguing us since the days of Adam and Eve, will be broken: "He will wipe away every tear from their eyes. Death will be no more; grief, crying, and pain will be no more, because the previous things have passed away" (Rev. 21:4).

In September 2021, my dad died. After heart surgery, he had spent a month and a half in the ICU—his body shutting down one system after another until his heart gave out. We were all in the room that day. Even at age forty, it was the first time I had really seen death up close, and I found myself suddenly understanding something about death that I had not understood before. As God's Word attests, death is not a beautiful "circle of life" moment but a terrible *enemy*. It's unnatural, an uprooting, a wrenching. It does not feel right because it is not how it's supposed to be. All around us, death continues to cast its shadows: miscarriage, disease, natural disaster, war, the body breaking down with age, and even the common cold reminds us that this enemy—though defeated in Christ—has yet to be fully destroyed. And so we ache for the day when God will crush death at last, swallowing it up once and for all.[7]

Still, death's defeat—though glorious—is not our deepest, truest longing.

EDEN'S PROMISE FULFILLED

In the new Jerusalem, John also sees God's abundant, beautiful work of creation—inaugurated in Eden—now expanding to cover the whole earth. We remember that a river flowed through Eden, watering the garden (Gen. 2:10). But God's garden city has something even *better*: a crystal "river of the water of life" flowing from the throne of God, a living water nourishing all who drink (Rev. 22:1–2). In Eden, diverse and delicious fruit weighed down the branches of countless trees, but the new Jerusalem has something *more*: a "tree of life was on each side of the river, bearing twelve kinds of fruit, producing its fruit every month. The leaves of the tree are for healing the nations" (Rev. 22:2). Nothing will be cursed in Zion; no thorn of sin or sorrow will be allowed to take root and grow. The city itself *radiates*, bedecked in gold, pearl, jasper, sapphire, and a myriad of other jewels. In exile, we remember that God's people faced thorns and briers, ashes and ruin, a dark wilderness. But here we see a new creation brimming over with light and life! If the devastation of exile was like *Eden undone*, the new Jerusalem will be like *exile undone*. Can you imagine it?

Still, this Edenic city—though beautiful—is not our deepest, truest longing.

GOD MAKES HIS HOME WITH US

Our deepest, truest longing is not for a place or even for the perpetuity of eternal life but for a *person.*

In his vision of heaven, John hears a thundering voice coming from the throne: "Look, God's dwelling is with humanity, and *he* will live with them. They will be *his* peoples, and God *himself* will be with them and will be their God" (Rev. 21:3, emphasis added).

Throughout the story of Scripture, we see God intending to make his home with us. He dwells with his people in the garden of Eden, then through the tabernacle and temple. During Advent, we look back on the birth of Emmanuel, "God with us" through the person of Jesus. And even now, God is making his home in his church through the Holy Spirit's indwelling. The Bible shows us that God is *always* making a way to be with us, even in our sin and exile. And in the new Jerusalem, God's intention to dwell with his people will be realized in full. *At last!*

One day God's expansive, glorious presence will saturate the new heavens and the new earth like the morning sun suffuses a dark room with its light. "The earth shall be *full* of the knowledge of the LORD as the waters cover the sea" (Isa. 11:9 ESV, emphasis added). There will be no need for a temple, for the whole city will be like the holy of holies! There will be no need for the light of the sun or moon because Jesus will shine like a lamp, and the glory of God will illuminate everything we see (Rev. 21:22–23)!

This Advent we long for death to be defeated. We ache for Eden to be restored. But more than anything, we are yearning for *God himself*. Hear the promise of Jesus: "Yes, I am coming soon." Then, take up this Advent prayer: "Amen! Come, Lord Jesus!"

RESPOND IN PRACTICE

Listen to "Behold, Behold (Revelation)" and try as best you can to imagine the scenes John describes in Revelation 21–22. Put yourself there. It is more beautiful, more vibrant, more colorful than anything you have ever experienced. Imagine your senses awake, your heart full of worship, your hands busy with good work. You are beloved of God, his beautiful *poiēma*, surrounded by the beauty of new creation and by the ransomed, singing saints. No more homesickness, for you are home. Won't it just be amazing?

Holding this image, respond to God in prayer.

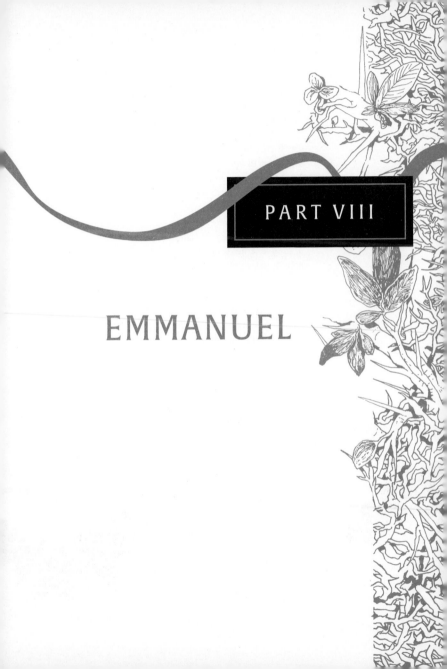

PART VIII

EMMANUEL

Blessed seed of Abraham
Born the nations now to bless
Promised son of mother Eve
Come to crush the serpent's head

Christ the sinless lamb of God
Every law in him complete
Slain to ransom rebel hearts
Raised for us a great high priest

He is here, he is here!
Emmanuel, God draws near
At long last, he has come!
Emmanuel, the Promised One

Isaiah's servant suffering
By his wounds we are healed
Son of Man in Daniel's dream
Glorious myst'ry now revealed

King of kings on David's throne
His rule and reign will never end
He will bring the exiles home
When his advent comes again

The one the prophets longed to know
The first, the last, the cornerstone!
Every promise finds its yes in him!
The Spirit with us til we sing this song again

He is here, he is here!
Emmanuel, God draws near
At long last, he has come!
Emmanuel, the Promised One

"Emmanuel (Every Promise Yes in Him),"
by Caroline Cobb

DAY 25

At Long Last, He Is Here!

On Christmas morning, all the waiting and anticipation should yield to glad enjoyment at last. All the ache and hunger—Advent's whetting of the appetite—give way to great feasting! All our watching for Jesus is fulfilled as we gaze into the face of our infant King.

The Seed promised to Adam and Eve is *here*! The Son promised to Abraham is *here*! The Passover Lamb who will lead us into the new exodus is *here*! The King of kings who reigns forever on David's throne is *here*! Isaiah's Righteous Branch and suffering Messiah is *here*! He is Emmanuel, God with us, the Word made flesh to dwell among us.

Today, do not hold back. Enjoy and savor and sing! Smile big and laugh hard as the children run into the room, rip back the wrapping paper, and happily revel in their gifts. Go ahead and be childlike too. Revel in gifts received and given, remembering God's better Gift. Worship the God who would come down to us in our exile. Feast with your loved ones! Be glad.

Let all these bright shafts of light point you beyond this happy morning and into the radiant light of eternal day. There we will feast with the family of God and see our King face-to-face! There we will enjoy the gift of the gospel to the full.

And, by the way, did you know you don't have to stop rejoicing after today? On the church calendar, Christmas is meant to last not one but *twelve* full days. That's twelve days of feasting, celebrating, and gifts. Twelve days of worship and grateful joy. Twelve days of rehearsing for the new Eden, where we will live in God's presence forever.

But what of the discontentment and dissonance we know will inevitably creep into this Christmas Day and the twelve days to follow? Even these signs of exile, these thorns and pangs of longing, can point you forward to gospel hope. When the toys break or run out of batteries, when the chair of a loved one sits empty, when the family conflicts bubble to the surface, when the malaise sets in—let these dark shadows sharpen your longing for the radiant city of Zion and for the King who will be her light.

Get up! Get ready! He is just around the bend!

RESPOND IN PRACTICE

Today, take note of the light and the
dark. The beauty and the brokenness.
The "already" and the "not yet." Then,
as you get into bed tonight, look back on
the day in a posture of prayer. What light
and beauty can you spend time thanking
him for? What shadows and brokenness
about the day can you bring to him in
prayer? Is there sin you need to confess
or an apology you need to make? How
do all of these things lead you to look
forward to Christ's second advent?

EPILOGUE

When I first read Tolkien's Lord of the Rings trilogy, I was surprised to find that the story does not end with the hobbits' destruction of the evil Ring of Power or with King Aragorn's victory over Lord Sauron. Instead, Tolkien spends an additional six chapters describing what happens next. Samwise returns to the Shire and begins to put things right: clearing out the darkness, releasing prisoners, restoring the wreckage the cursed ring had wrought in his homeland. Aragon establishes his reign as a king marked by mercy and justice, bringing healing and goodness to Gondor's capital city, and planting a new sapling tree in the royal courtyard as a sign of a new age of flourishing and joy.[1]

In the same way, Jesus's arrival on Christmas Day is not the end of the story. As we have explored throughout this devotional, the birth, life, death, resurrection, and ascension of Christ have indeed inaugurated a new, Edenic kingdom, but that kingdom has yet to be fully realized. In this season between advents, God is working through his people to push back the darkness, to plant seeds of hope in the wilderness, to rebuild the ruins wrought by the curse of sin and death. Even as we celebrate the first advent of Christ, we continue to look to his second advent with hopeful anticipation.

When Jesus comes again on the last day, our story—in one sense—will come to a close. Our long exile will be over, the shadows and thorns expelled by the radiant beauty of God's presence. But, in another sense, our story will just be beginning. As C. S. Lewis writes at the end of his Chronicles of Narnia series: "All their life in this world and all their adventures in Narnia had only been the cover and the title page: now at last they were beginning Chapter One of the Great Story which no one on earth has read: which goes on forever: in which every chapter is better than the one before."[2]

In the season of Christmas, we are invited to look ahead with joy at "Chapter One of the Great Story." In our feasting and singing, we are rehearsing for the main show: that glad satisfaction we will find with God in his heavenly new Eden, where every chapter is better than the one before. We remember our exile here is just the cover and title page, and we wait expectantly for Christ's coming. *At last! At last!*

Acknowledgments

Although I have been writing songs and releasing albums for many years, writing my first book required a different kind of creative depth and patient endurance. As I stepped into this work for the first time, so many came alongside me to encourage me, pray for me, and guide me through to the finish line.

To my husband Nick: In each and every creative endeavor, you are a steady support, a constant source of wisdom, and a listening ear. When I run too hard, you help me slow my pace and remind me of why I create in the first place. Thank you for loving me as I am, before I produce a thing or write a word. I love you.

To Ellie, Harrison and Libby: I treasure each one of you deeply and, as I say often, I love being your mom. Thank you for your ongoing patience and sacrifice as I spent many hours writing this book, and as I continue to look for ways to create beauty for God's glory. I love all three of you so dearly, and I cannot wait to see how our loving Father continues to shape you into his image.

To our local church, White Rock Fellowship: Thank you for supporting me in so many ways and for sending me with your blessing and prayers into the work of music, and now writing. To all those who have supported my creative projects in the past, and especially to the current community of patrons on Patreon: Thank you for enabling me to continue to tell the Story as faithfully and beautifully as I can. I could not do this kind of work without your backing, and I do not take it for granted.

To our families: Thank you for always rooting for me, coming to concerts, generously offering childcare, and so much more. And to my friends, especially the "advisory board" of 2021 and others who have prayed for me and spoken encouragement over me in seasons of weariness and angst: thank you for spurring me on, for resonating with the work I put into the world, for re-centering me when I want to quit, and reminding me of what's true when I forget.

To my editor Ashley Gorman: Thank you for catching a vision for this book from the very beginning, and for helping me shape my words and ideas into *Advent for Exiles*. And thank you for assuring me that I could indeed write—not just songs, but a whole book too. Your confidence meant the world. To artist Stephen Procopio and the entire B&H design team: Thank you for your attention to detail and for adding so much beauty to this book. To my literary agent Don Gates and the writer friends who helped me find my way as a new author: I am grateful. To the earliest readers: Nick, Andi, Jeff and Lori, Christine, Erica, and Haley, thank you for wading through my roughest draft, and telling me I should try to get it published.

God, thank you for allowing me to write and sing about you. Your Word is beautiful and true, and we could never plumb the depths of your goodness. *Soli Deo Gloria.*

About the Author

Before her thirtieth birthday, Caroline Cobb set a goal to write a song for every book of the Bible in one year. That year set a new calling into motion: to tell God's Story through music and other creative work, helping you rehearse it and respond to it as you go about your everyday life.

Her most recent album, *Psalms: The Poetry of Prayer* (May 2023) gives voice to a rich range of prayers from the Psalms, and builds on Caroline's previous "Story-telling" projects *A King & His Kindness* (2021), *A Seed, A Sunrise* (2020), a *Home & a Hunger* (2017), and *the Blood + the Breath* (2013).

Caroline has been featured by *Christianity Today*, The Gospel Coalition, The Rabbit Room, Risen Motherhood, and many more, with a *Home & a Hunger* named among "The Best Albums of the Decade (2010's)" by The Gospel Coalition. She and her husband Nick live in Dallas with their three children Ellie, Harrison, and Libby.

Notes

Preface

1. I originally wrestled through these ideas in an article for The Gospel Coalition. Caroline Cobb, "2020 Has Felt like Advent All Year," The Gospel Coalition, November 23, 2020, https://www.thegospelcoalition.org/article/2020-has-felt-like-advent-all-year.

2. Cobb, "2020 Has Felt like Advent All Year."

Introduction

1. Fleming Rutledge, *Advent: The Once and Future Coming of Jesus Christ* (Grand Rapids: William B. Eerdmans, 2018), 5–6.

2. Rutledge, *Advent*, 7.

3. While most of the daily Scripture readings were based on the texts that originally inspired the selected song lyrics, some were shaped by the Advent lectionary included in *The Book of Common Prayer* (Huntington Beach, CA: Anglican Liturgy Press, 2019).

4. Some scholars believe Isaiah was written by at least two authors over a span of two hundred years. In this view, Isaiah 1–39 was written by the prophet himself, and the rest of the book was written by a prophet alive during the Babylonian exile. Although I do not pretend to be a biblical scholar and do not say this explicitly, this devotional book tends toward the view that the entirety of the book of Isaiah was written by Isaiah himself.

5. Emily Dickinson, "Tell All the Truth but Tell It Slant" in *The Poems of Emily Dickinson*, ed. by R. W. Franklin (Cambridge, MA: Harvard University Press, 1999).

6. C. S. Lewis, *Selected Literary Essays* (Cambridge: Cambridge University Press, 2013), 265.

7. Caroline Cobb, "Tell That Story," track 1 on *Tell That Story EP*, Sing the Story Music, November 2019.

Part I: The First Exile

1. Meredith G. Kline, *Kingdom Prologue: Genesis Foundations for a Covenantal Worldview* (Eugene, OR: Wipf and Stock, 2006), 43.

2. This idea was first introduced to me throughout Gloria Furman's book on Ephesians, *Alive in Him*, especially pages 80–81. Gloria Furman, *Alive in Him: How Being Embraced by the Love of Christ Changes Everything* (Wheaton, IL: Crossway, 2017), 80–81.

3. Augustine, *Confessions*, trans. Henry Chadwick (Oxford: Oxford University Press, 1992), 1.1.1.

4. The idea of *homo incurvatus in se* is widespread, but it may have originated in Augustine or Martin Luther.

5. Emily Dickinson, "Success Is Counted Sweetest," in *The Poems of Emily Dickinson*, ed. by R. W. Franklin (Cambridge, MA: Harvard University Press, 1999).

Part II: In the Darkness of Exile, a Sunrise

1. Nancy Guthrie, *Even Better Than Eden: Nine Ways the Bible's Story Changes Everything about Your Story* (Wheaton, IL: Crossway, 2018), 133.

2. Michael D. Williams, *Far as the Curse Is Found* (Phillipsburg, NJ: P&R Publishers, 2005), 149.

3. These warnings are not new, and the exile should not be viewed as a sudden, reactive decision made by a quick-tempered God. Since the time of Moses, God has promised blessing for covenant obedience and curses for disobedience. For example, Deuteronomy 28:1–14 catalogs the blessings an obedient Israel will receive: the presence of God, victory over other nations, an abundance of harvest and livestock and even children, the people of God fulfilling the "be fruitful and multiply" command. The covenant kept results in Eden restored. Deuteronomy 28:15–68, on the other hand, catalogs the consequence of disobedience: diseases and scarcity; a land marred by scorching heat, drought and mildew; a God whose presence seems to be *against* them rather than for them and, as a culminating curse, the exile itself. See also 1 Chronicles 36:15–16.

4. J. R. R. Tolkien, *The Two Towers* (Boston: Mariner Books, 1994), 701–2.

5. Tolkien, *The Two Towers*, 704.

6. "O Come O Come Emmanuel," translated by John Mason Neale, in *Hymns Ancient and Modern*, ed. by William Henry Monk (London: Canterbury Press, 1861). Public Domain.

7. J. R. R. Tolkien, *The Return of the King* (Boston: Mariner Books, 1994), 930.

8. James Strong, *Strong's Expanded Exhaustive Concordance of the Bible* (Nashville: Thomas Nelson, 2009), s.v. "dwelt," John 1:14, Blue Letter Bible, https://blueletterbible.org/lexicon/g4637/kjv/tr/0-1/.

9. G. K. Beale and Michael Kim, *God Dwells among Us: Expanding Eden to the Ends of the Earth* (Downers Grove, IL: InterVarsity Press, 2014), 82.

10. "Joy to the World," text by Isaac Watts (1719). Public Domain.

11. Sandra L. Richter, *The Epic of Eden: A Christian Entry into the Old Testament* (Downers Grove, IL: InterVarsity Press, 2008), 182.

12. The idea of Jesus taking the blow of the cherubim's sword came to my attention in Tim Keller's book on the gospel of Mark, *King's Cross*. Timothy Keller, *King's Cross: The Story of the World in the Life of Jesus* (New York: Dutton, 2011), 159.

13. J. R. R. Tolkien, *The Letters of J. R. R. Tolkien*, ed. by H. Carpenter and C. Tolkien (Boston: Houghton Mifflin, 2000), 110.

14. Gerard Manley Hopkins, "God's Grandeur," in *Gerard Manley Hopkins: Poems and Prose,* ed. by W. H. Gardner (London: Penguin Classics, 1985).

15. C. S. Lewis, *The Weight of Glory and Other Addresses* (New York: Harper Collins, 1980).

16. The whole section is worth quoting in full: "Probably earthly pleasures were never meant to satisfy it, but only to arouse it, to suggest the real thing. If that is so, I must take care, on the one hand, never to despise, or be unthankful for, these earthly blessings, and on the other, never to mistake them for the something else of which they are only a kind of copy, or echo, or mirage. I must keep alive in myself the desire for my true country, which I shall not find till after death; I must never let it get snowed under or turned aside; I must make it the main object of life to press on to that other country and to help others to do

the same." C. S. Lewis, *Mere Christianity* (New York: Harper Collins, 1980), 136–37.

Part III: In the Wilderness of Exile, a Seed and a Highway

1. Shelby Vittek, "A Beginner's Guide to Growing Your Own Wine Grapes," Modern Farmer, July 18, 2021, https://modernfarmer.com/2021/07/a-beginners-guide-to-growing-your-own-wine-grapes. See also Marvin P. Pritts, "Growing Grapes in the Home Garden," Cornell Cooperative Extension, May 1996, https://chemung.cce.cornell.edu/resources/growing-grapes-in-the-home-garden.

2. J. Alec Motyer, *The Prophecy of Isaiah: An Introduction and Commentary* (Downers Grove, IL: InterVarsity Press, 1993), 68.

3. Another song that interacts with these ideas is Andrew Peterson's "Sower's Song." Andrew Peterson, "Sower's Song," track 10 on *The Burning Edge of Dawn*, Centricity Music, October 2015.

4. L. Michael Morales, *Exodus Old and New: A Biblical Theology of Redemption* (Downers Grove, IL: InterVarsity Press, 2020), 119.

5. Morales, *Exodus Old and New*, 119.

6. Nancy Guthrie's book *Even Better Than Eden* first introduced me to this concept. Nancy Guthrie, *Even Better Than Eden: Nine Ways the Bible's Story Changes Everything about Your Story* (Wheaton, IL: Crossway, 2018).

7. Motyer, *The Prophecy of Isaiah*, 273–75, 404.

Part IV: For the Lost Sheep in Exile, a Shepherd-King

1. Sandra L. Richter, *The Epic of Eden: A Christian Entry into the Old Testament* (Downers Grove, IL: InterVarsity Press, 2008), 196.

2. Richter, *The Epic of Eden*, 203.

3. Revelation 22:16 adds to this conversation. Jesus states, "I am the Root and descendant of David, the bright morning star." Jesus is *both* the root and the offspring or seed of Jesse. He is the source and the budding branch.

4. Tim Mackie, "Isaiah's Anointed One," *The Bible Project*, Podcast Audio, April 3, 2023, https://bibleproject.com/podcast/isaiahs-anointed-one.

5. Craig G. Bartholomew and Michael W. Goheen, *The Drama of Scripture: Finding Our Place in the Biblical Story* (Grand Rapids, MI: Baker Academic, 2014), 131–37.

6. A. W. Tozer, *The Knowledge of the Holy* (New York: HarperCollins, 1961), 3.

7. J. Alec Motyer, *The Prophecy of Isaiah: An Introduction and Commentary* (Downers Grove, IL: InterVarsity Press, 1993), 300.

8. Albert Barnes, "Commentary on Isaiah 40: Barnes' Notes on the Whole Bible," StudyLight.org, accessed December 21, 2023, https://www.studylight.org/commentaries/eng/bnb/isaiah-40.html.

9. Fleming Rutledge, *Advent: The Once and Future Coming of Jesus Christ* (Grand Rapids: William B. Eerdmans, 2018), 315.

Part V: In the Silence of Exile, the Word of God

1. Hope A. Blanton and Christine B. Gordon, *Luke: Part 1: A Study of Luke–8* (Omaha: 19Baskets, 2019), 25.

2. John Milton, "This Is the Month," in *The Soul in Paraphrase: A Treasury of Classic Devotional Poems*, ed. Leland Ryken (Wheaton: Crossway, 2018), 232.

3. Alexander Stewart and Andreas J. Köstenberger, *The First Days of Jesus: The Story of the Incarnation* (Wheaton, IL: Crossway, 2015), 147.

4. Stewart and Köstenberger, *The First Days of Jesus*, 148.

5. Darrell L. Bock argues that Jesus was not following a fixed reading plan, but intentionally chose this particular text from Isaiah. Bock also writes that Luke might be intentionally summarizing a longer citation, with his abbreviated version here drawn primarily from Isaiah 61:1–2a but also, probably, from Isaiah 58:6. Both chapters touch on the idea of Jubilee. Darrell L. Bock, *Luke Volume 1: Baker Exegetical Commentary on the New Testament* ed. Moisés Silva (Grand Rapids, MI: Baker Academic, 1994), 404–13.

6. Bock, *Luke Volume 1: Baker Exegetical Commentary on the New Testament*, 411–12.

7. J. Alec Motyer, *The Prophecy of Isaiah: An Introduction and Commentary* (Downers Grove, IL: InterVarsity Press, 1993), 499–500.

8. Nancy Guthrie, *The One Year Book of Discovering Jesus in the Old Testament* (Carol Stream, IL: Tyndale House Publishers, 2010), 295.

9. Caroline Cobb, "There Is a Mountain," track 1 on *A Home & a Hunger,* Sing the Story Music, September 2017.

Part VI: In the Ashes and Ruin of Exile, a New Home for God

1. Charles Haddon Spurgeon, "Commentary on Isaiah 61: Spurgeon's Verse Expositions of the Bible," StudyLight.org, accessed December 23, 2023, https://www.studylight.org/commentaries/eng/spe/isaiah-61.html.2011.

2. J. Alec Motyer, *The Prophecy of Isaiah: An Introduction and Commentary* (Downers Grove, IL: InterVarsity Press, 1993), 500–501.

3. Spurgeon, "Commentary on Isaiah 61: Spurgeon's Verse Expositions of the Bible."

4. Spurgeon, "Commentary on Isaiah 61: Spurgeon's Verse Expositions of the Bible."

5. For more on this painting and the story of the prodigal from Luke 15, see Henri Nouwen's moving book *Return of the Prodigal Son.* Henri J. M. Nouwen, *Return of the Prodigal Son: A Story of Homecoming* (New York: Doubleday, 1992).

6. Ray Ortlund, "Our Mission: Making the Real Jesus Non-Ignorable in Our City and Far Beyond (Isaiah 61)," Sermon for Immanuel Nashville, November 4, 2012.

7. C. S. Lewis, *Mere Christianity* (New York: Harper Collins, 1980), 142.

8. Joseph Hart, "Come Ye Sinners Poor and Needy" (1759). Public Domain.

9. *The ESV Study Bible, English Standard Version (ESV)* (Wheaton, IL: Crossway, 2008), 1876.

10. Fleming Rutledge, *Advent: The Once and Future Coming of Jesus Christ* (Grand Rapids: Eerdmans, 2018), 92.

11. For a sampling of Paul's use of the light-versus-dark motif, see Ephesians 5:7–8; 6:12; Romans 2:19; 13:1–12; Colossians 1:13–14; 2 Corinthians 6:14; 1 Thessalonians 5:2–8.

12. T. S. Eliot, "The Journey of the Magi," in *The Soul in Paraphrase: A Treasury of Classic Devotional Poems*, ed. Leland Ryken (Wheaton, IL: Crossway, 2018), 221–23.

13. Rutledge, *Advent*, 54.

14. N. T. Wright, *Surprised by Hope: Rethinking Heaven, the Resurrection, and the Mission of the Church* (New York: HarperCollins, 2008), 208–9.

15. I became familiar with this phrase through Eugene Peterson's book of the same name, but Peterson pulled it from Friedrich Nietzsche, *Beyond Good and Evil*. Eugene Peterson, *A Long Obedience in the Same Direction: Discipleship in an Instant Society* (Downers Grove, IL: InterVarsity Press, 2000).

Part VII: In Our Present Exile, a Future Hope

1. J. Alec Motyer, *The Prophecy of Isaiah: An Introduction and Commentary* (Downers Grove, IL: InterVarsity Press, 1993), 54.

2. Tim Mackie, "Exile from the Cosmic Mountain," The Bible Project, Podcast Audio, February 14, 2018, https://bibleproject.com/podcast/exile-cosmic-mountain.

3. G. K. Beale and Michael Kim, *God Dwells among Us: Expanding Eden to the Ends of the Earth* (Downers Grove, IL: InterVarsity Press, 2014), 18. See also The Bible Project Podcast.

4. See Nancy Guthrie, *Even Better Than Eden: Nine Ways the Bible's Story Changes Everything about Your Story* (Wheaton, IL: Crossway, 2018); as well as Beale and Kim, *God Dwells among Us*. See also Hebrews 12:18–24 for a comparison of Sinai and Zion.

5. Barry G. Webb, *The Message of Isaiah* (Downers Grove, IL: Intervarsity Press, 1997), 76.

6. Motyer, *The Prophecy of Isaiah*, 54.

7. My recent thinking on these concepts has been formed by Tish Harrison Warren's *Prayer in the Night*, a book I began reading just days after my dad's funeral. Tish Harrison Warren, *Prayer in the Night* (Downer's Grove, IL: InterVarsity Press, 2021), 116–17.

Epilogue

1. J. R. R. Tolkien, *The Return of the King* (Boston: Mariner Books, 1994), 927–97.

2. C. S. Lewis, *The Last Battle* (New York: HarperCollins, 1884), 210–11.

Enjoy More Holiday Offerings from B&H

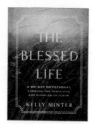

Similar Authors or Books You Might Like

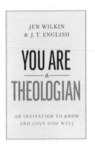  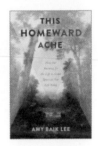

  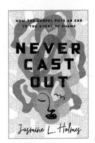

Available where books are sold.

find more from **Caroline Cobb**

Caroline Cobb has a heart to tell God's Story through music and other creative work, helping listeners and readers like you remember, rehearse and respond to it. Over the last ten years, she has released five full-length albums and over 50 songs from scripture, with hopes to continue to write, sing and create for God's glory. Come, dive deeper and follow along.

Psalms: The Poetry of Prayer

An album giving voice to a rich range of prayers from the Psalms, helping you express trust, hope, joy, confession, lament and more through 11 tracks. Featuring Jess Ray (Mission House), Aaron Fabbrini (Sara Groves, Jason Gray), and Wendell Kimbrough and patterned loosely after the A.C.T.S. model of prayer or a church service, many of these songs began during Cobb's private devotional time, as she prayed the Psalms back to God in the upheaval of 2020.

A King & His Kindness
an intimate portrait of Jesus

A Seed, A Sunrise
songs for Advent to Christmas

the Blood + the Breath
the arc of redemption

A Home & A Hunger
the "already but not yet"